Points North and East

Front cover picture:
Peggy's Cove, Nova Scotia
Photo Janet Barclay

Rear cover picture:
Somewhere on HWY 510, Labrador
Photo Janet Barclay

Points North and East

Janet Barclay

Loose Cannon Press

LIBRARY AND ARCHIVES CANADA CATALOGUING IN PUBLICATION

Barclay, Janet, 1947-, author
Points north and east / Janet Barclay.

ISBN 978-0-9936881-8-8 (paperback)

1. Barclay, Janet, 1947- —Travel. 2. Newfoundland and Labrador—Description and travel. 3. Maritime Provinces—Description and travel. I. Title.

FC2167.6.B37 2015 917.1804'5 C2015-906378-7

Published by
LOOSE CANNON PRESS

info@loosecannonpress.com
www.loosecannonpress.com

Table of Contents

Acknowledgements vi
One: Introduction 1
Two: Ottawa to Labrador City 5
Three: Labrador City and Goose Bay 23
Four: Happy Valley-Goose Bay to Hopedale 39
Five: Hopedale, Nain and Back 57
Six: Goose Bay to Red Bay 79
Seven: Red Bay to Blanc Sablon 97
Eight: Blanc Sablon to L'Anse aux Meadows 111
Nine: St Anthony to Twillingate 129
Ten: Twillingate to Terra Nova 143
Eleven: Terra Nova to Bonavista 159
Twelve: Bonavista to Argentia 177
Thirteen: Cape Breton 199
Fourteen: Chéticamp to Pictou 219
Fifteen: Prince Edward Island 233
Sixteen: More of Prince Edward Island 249
Seventeen: New Brunswick and Home 265
Resources 274
I'se the B'y 275
The Ballad of Springhill 276

Acknowledgements

I would like to thank all those people we met on our travels who shared their stories with us, and who made our voyage of discovery that much more interesting and rewarding. Special thanks go to our friends who allowed us to park in their driveways during our explorations of the Maritimes, and entertained us while doing so. I acknowledge the friendliness and support of the staff at Ottawa Camping Trailers. Thanks also to my husband Bob for all his support and encouragement in making this book a reality.

Chapter One
Introduction

After many years of tent camping, we became the proud owners of a small RV in 2010, and this has given us the opportunity to explore many places throughout Canada and the USA. In 2012 we found our way up to Inuvik and Alaska (see *Points North and West* in Resources, p. 274) and having experienced this eight-week odyssey we were anxious and excited to start another long trip. So after traveling through the western and northern parts of this amazing country, we decided in 2014 that the East Coast required a closer look. After consulting the map and checking the tourist information supplied by all the Maritime Provinces we decided to make Labrador our first destination, and to take the passenger/cargo ship up the coast to Nain. The five-day voyage, starting and finishing in Happy Valley-Goose Bay, would enable us to visit those areas of the province not really accessible in the summer, except by sea or air. We needed to allow the five days of shipboard traveling, and the idea of having the opportunity to see several of the settlements along the coast was most intriguing. So we quickly booked that voyage and then started loosely planning the rest of our travels around those dates.

Since we wanted to have time to explore both Labrador and Newfoundland, as well as the other eastern provinces, we estimated this trip would likely take us about six weeks. Even so, we both understood we would only be touching the surface of what the Maritimes have to offer, but we knew we would come away with some new experiences and memories.

After Newfoundland and Labrador, our next priority would be Prince Edward Island since I had never had a chance to visit this appealing place, and friends from Ottawa had recently moved there. Then Nova Scotia needed to be revisited, with the chance of catching up with other friends from home who were now living there. Finally, we planned to make a brief stop in New Brunswick, meet friends in Saint John, and spend a day or so exploring that area of the province. So, with these tentative plans in mind we studied the tourist information books of the various provinces and from the Canadian Automobile Association

(CAA), all of which increased our anticipation and excitement about this trip. Then the serious planning began.

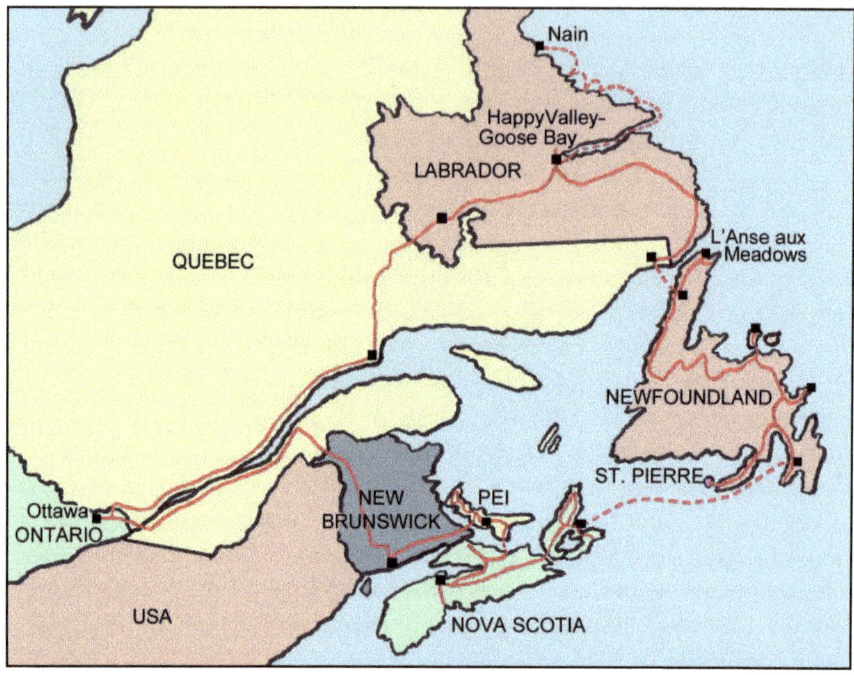

The map of our entire journey. At the head of each chapter a map will show each section of the route in detail

First things first, we booked the coastal voyage to Nain, and with that deadline in mind we figured on about one week of travel just to get to Happy Valley-Goose Bay at the rate we usually travel. Then, how much time did we need to tour around Labrador? Allow another week. Then the ferry to Newfoundland itself; not sure when that would be, so book it while on our travels. As our planning went along in this way we began to set approximate dates of our meetings with friends in Nova Scotia, PEI and New Brunswick. When all of these contacts were made, and tentative arrival times established, it was time to plan for the trip itself.

Following our trip to the north and west in 2012 we had learned so much more, which gave us a better idea of our specific requirements for traveling in such a small space and over an extended length of time. It really wasn't about the major things in life, but rather those small things that can become annoying. For a perhaps trivial example, we made sure this time to bring a couple of small shampoo containers with us for use in the campground showers! Leaving the new bottle of shampoo in a shower stall and not realizing it until the next stop can be frustrating! We have done this often enough to know. Then, the grandchildren like to receive postcards, so self-adhesive address labels can be printed out beforehand to make life easier when posting. Electronic devices will insist on being charged at various times—which I believe is most inconsiderate of them—so all their various and non-interchangeable chargers must be on board. We once left the power supply for the laptop at home, which necessitated a visit to a local store for a replacement one. Not the most convenient thing to happen. As a result, long lists based on experience were made to make ensure that everything was ready for the big day.

As our departure date came closer we had one last thing to do; contact our friends living near Mont Tremblant in Quebec to check if we could drop in to see them on our way. So, with all this in mind we left Ottawa after lunch one day, pointed the van east, and started on the first short leg of this new adventure.

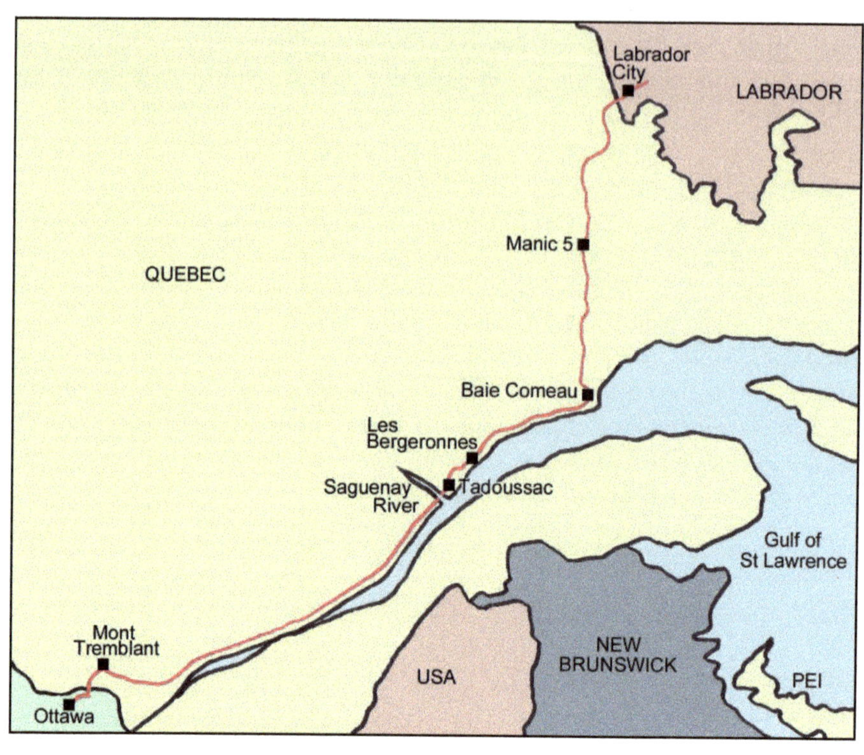

Ottawa to Mt Tremblant	200km
Mt Tremblant to Les Bergeronnes	648km
Les Bergeronnes to Manic 5	481km
Manic 5 to Labrador City	467km
TOTAL	1796km

Chapter Two
Ottawa to Labrador City

During our preparations we reminisced on many of our previous travels in the RV, and wondered how this one would compare. The trip to the northern and western parts of Canada, and into Alaska was something never to be forgotten; our very first long distance drive to Florida for a week in the winter was pretty special; the trip without water due to a broken hot water tank (it leaked whenever the water was switched on!); and how about touring around the Niagara wine region? Those trips and many more held so many memories, and now we hoped to add many more on this, our second longest trip. Even knowing we had had several successful trips under our belt, as we left home on this new adventure, we still had a slight feeling of trepidation along with the anticipation of the journey. What wonderful things would we see and learn about? What disasters awaited us in the wings? Would we make all the connections and visit all the places we had planned? These were only some of our thoughts as we drove out of our driveway. We were almost sure we had anticipated as much we could, so now it was time to get going and enjoy the journey.

Leaving Ottawa we knew our first day of driving would be fairly easy, since our first stop was at a friend's house near Mont Tremblant in Quebec. On these adventures we find it very useful to use our GPS, fondly known to us as Madame GPS. So when she led us to the ferry crossing the Ottawa River between Cumberland and Masson we were rather amused because the highway through Ottawa and into Gatineau was the main highway. This was to be the first ferry crossing of the five we were to encounter on this road trip. This first one only took us five minutes, and was also therefore one of the shortest of crossings of our travels. As we crossed the river we reminisced on that never-to-be-forgotten crossing of the Peel River in the Northwest Territories. That particular crossing took about the same time as this one, the only difference being the long line-up of vehicles waiting for the ferry ramps to be rebuilt! The ramps had been washed out by a storm, and the actual time to wait for the ferry crossing had been measured in days!

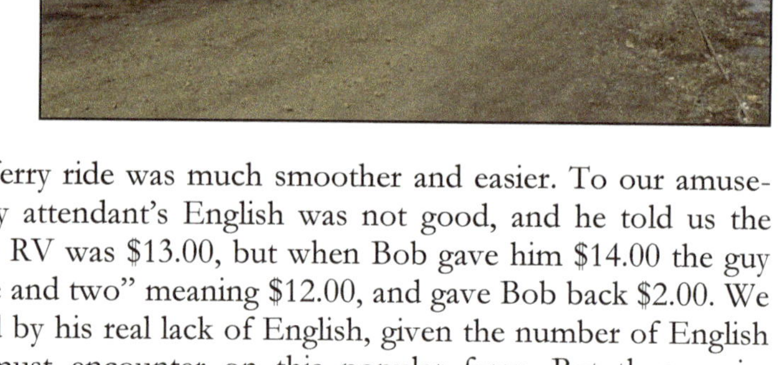

Contrasting ferries: the Ottawa River and the Peel River under construction

This present ferry ride was much smoother and easier. To our amusement the ferry attendant's English was not good, and he told us the charge for the RV was $13.00, but when Bob gave him $14.00 the guy said, "No, one and two" meaning $12.00, and gave Bob back $2.00. We were surprised by his real lack of English, given the number of English speakers he must encounter on this popular ferry. But then again, perhaps not, given my deficits in our second official language.

This was an easy day of driving, other than the discrepancy between our friend's directions and those of Madame GPS. We realized after we arrived at our destination that Madame had taken us the long way around, and brought us to the house via a very attractive lake. While it may have taken us a little extra time to get to the cottage, Madame's route showed us the easiest way back to the highway for the next stage of this adventure.

With good friends (right) at the start of our trip

The cottage was very lovely, and the company even better, and we caught up with all the current news over dinner and wine. After supper we went back to our little home on wheels for our first night on the road. It was at the end of this first day on the road we began to appreciate that, while we didn't have to travel as far to reach the east coast in contrast to traveling west, we still had three days of solid driving before we would arrive in Labrador and start the exciting part of our trip.

We left our friends soon after breakfast and headed east and thankfully by-passing Montreal to the north on our way towards Quebec City. After a brief stop at Bennies, a very convenient rest stop between Montreal and Quebec City, it was on towards Quebec City and points further east. Happily, the highway by-passes Quebec City itself as well, so we were able to travel quite fast and very easily. We were aiming for the ferry at Tadoussac, and initially hoped to find a campground for the night and then cross the Saguenay River the next day. However, we encountered very few campgrounds along the North Shore and, as so often happens in our travels, we changed plans in mid-stream—or perhaps mid-road would be more appropriate—deciding to cross over on the ferry and stop for the night on the other side.

The road was enjoyable because, as it followed the North Shore of the St Lawrence River, it crossed many rivers entering from the north. This reminded us of our old mantra from the Alaska Highway: Down, down, down, across a bridge and then up, up, up, with the addition of sharp curves at either end of the process. (And, of course, there was no shoreline along the Alaska Highway.) We were laughing at ourselves as we reminisced about that earlier trip, and compared the differences between the Quebec landscape and that of the northern areas. Instead of the mountains and rather stark terrain of the north, we traveled along the softer coastline and through some delightful seacoast villages. We wondered about the people of the area and the stories they could tell. Many months later I was chatting with a charming lady I chanced to meet about our experiences driving through this area. Much to my surprise and interest she had lived there as a child, and had spent many happy times with her grandparents, especially her grandfather who was a salmon fisherman. She recalled on one occasion, as a very young child, she and her cousin went out to the beach early in the morning, just as the tide was going down, and they found the nets were absolutely full of fish. They ran back to the house and her grandfather and others from the village returned with them to the beach to collect this amazing catch. As I reflected on her tale, it gave me a new sense of the area; one I wished I had known as we drove along the shoreline.

We finally arrived at the ferry, which brought back so many memories of me as a young adult, traveling to England on a cargo ship to start my training as a nurse, having left my friends and parents at home in Trinidad. I didn't know enough of the world to worry about being a young single girl on a cargo vessel, and had just set out to enjoy the trip. The ship was carrying bauxite up to Lac St Jean on the Saguenay River. After off-loading it proceeded to Montreal to collect the next cargo destined for Bristol in England, its final port of call and the end of my personal adventures. I really enjoyed the trip, and although it took nearly one month, I would happily travel that way again.

The ferry across the Saguenay River

Revisiting the Saguenay after a lapse of so many years

After leaving the ferry it didn't take us long to find a nice campsite, Bon Desire near Les Bergeronnes. This very pretty campground is right on the shoreline and after a relaxing supper we took a walk beside the water and generally enjoyed the peace it provided. It was a perfect start to the true beginning of our travels.

Following an early start next morning we headed towards Baie Comeau and Highway 389, the official start of the road to Labrador. We continued along the shoreline, up and down, while enjoying the ever-changing scenery, until we arrived in Baie Comeau. As is our usual pattern when traveling, we found the Information Centre and went in right away to learn more about the road to Labrador City. A very helpful staff member provided us with a map especially produced for travelers on the only drivable road to Labrador City, and told us a little about it. We spent some time examining the map and the various descriptors of it, confirming that the road was both gravel and asphalt, and described as narrow and winding, with many steep parts along the way. Well, in our naivety, we thought, "We have driven the Dempster Highway from Dawson City to Inuvik in not very good conditions, so how much worse could this be?" We were also provided with easy directions to Highway 389, so after a brief stop for gas, we were on our way.

As we confidently started on a nicely paved road we should have remembered our experience with the Dempster Highway. That road started off with a nicely paved stretch, but it wasn't long before it deteriorated into gravel and mud. This road was no different; the nicely paved section at the beginning was merely a teaser. It soon became apparent that there was no relaxing. Cruise control became nothing more than a dream as we negotiated the RV around and through the frequent tight bends and twists on this very narrow road. Not content with negotiating difficult terrain, the road had also fallen apart in many areas, and although it had been patched many times, it was in dire need of the loving attention of a paving crew. As we—and the pots and pans and everything else that could move—were bounced around, we wondered if a good gravel surface would have been easier to drive. Then, just as the bumping and jumping was becoming too much, we would find a kilometre of two of smooth asphalt, which lulled us into a false sense of security, since all too soon we were back to the 'normal' surface of the road.

We were aware of the importance of the hydroelectric dams in the area, and had read the information provided on them by the staff in Baie Comeau, so we were looking forward to seeing them. After what seemed like an eternity of negotiating the highway, we thankfully stopped at the first dam, Manic 2. We made lunch while watching the water pouring through the spillways. It was a spectacular site, but knew from the information we had been given that was the smaller of the two facilities accessible to the public. Having seen this one from the parking lot, and being totally in amazed by its size, we could only imagine what Manic 5, the larger one, would look like. We knew both facilities offered tours, so we decided to continue to Manic 5 and hope we would be in time for one of them.

Manic 2; spectacular, but the smaller of the ones we would visit

After this peaceful interlude we started on the road again and, amazingly, it had not improved during our lunch break. We came across construction areas in the many dips in the road, and it looked as if the crews were replacing culverts at the lower points. These areas were all gravel and mud, which we found easier to handle. The pauses for one-way stop lights gave us the opportunity to add more bungees to various cupboards and drawers to prevent them opening and spilling their contents all over the floor.

Road maintenance was a constant feature of this road

Apart from these inconveniences, the scenery all along the road was spectacular. It was mainly forest with lakes, streams and small rivers appearing and disappearing, while throughout the whole area we could see the massive towers transmitting the vast quantities of hydroelectric power to transformer stations and hence into the grid serving the whole of Eastern North America. We passed one huge transformer station and stopped briefly to look at it and take pictures. It was quite the sight, and made us realize how much infrastructure there is just to keep our lights on and our computers working. We take it all for granted and don't think about how this power is generated and transmitted.

A pleasant roadside scene, happily devoid of transmission towers

Now it was time to drive on to Manic 5. We arrived there at about 3:00pm and signed up for the last tour of the day. We had about 30 minutes to get ourselves organized for the tour and to find a campsite for the night. Fortunately the very helpful tour guides directed us to the Belvedere, an area owned by Hydro Quebec where we would be able to stay overnight at no charge. Understandably, it was an unserviced site, which was fine for us, and it was very close to the dam, making it made it very convenient. Once we had that assurance we were ready to enjoy the tour of the whole hydroelectric facility.

The dam itself is huge. The guidebook showed a variety of pictures comparing the dam to some well-known sites such as the Eiffel Tower, the Olympic Stadium in Montreal and several other notable structures. The dam dwarfed them all. Just peering up at the dam wall was truly awe inspiring, and had the effect of making us feel as small as ants when up against that huge expanse of concrete. It seemed incredible that it had been considered practical to build such a massive dam so far away from large centers of population. In retrospect, it had been one of those inspired ideas.

Manic 5. The pickup truck on the road gives an idea of scale

The tour would take us inside the workings of the facility, but first we were shown around the exhibition area. It was all in French, so as the only Anglophones we were given our own personal guide for this section. We were shown the large scale model of the dam and its surrounding structures, while our guide used the model to describe the building and operation of the dam. This gave us an idea of what was to come when the actual tour started. Once we were on the ancient school bus that would take us to the various facilities and the dam itself, we were provided with hardhats and shown how to wear them properly. After all, the thought of the ensuing chaos should a hardhat fall into the machinery just didn't bear thinking about! We were given a guide book in English, which helped us follow along with the tour.

The first stop was the turbine floor and while we couldn't actually see them, we could certainly hear those huge pieces of machinery humming under our feet. Then it was down to the level where the water entered the system through huge pipes, and finally we were shown where the water left the system and flowed downstream, having expended its energy. It was interesting to learn about the other dams in this system. The Manicougan River passes through multiple generating stations in the system as it flows from one dam to the next, until it reaches the end of the system nearly at the St Lawrence River. So the same water is used over and over again. Altogether, the water passes through four dams in the system, producing electricity from each one. Talk about recycling! We were surprised to learn that the hydroelectric dam system in Quebec provides enough power to meet 99% of the demand of the province, and the last 1% is purchased from wind farms. And, in addition to supplying the province, Hydro Quebec is also able to sell power to the North American grid.

After visiting the generating facility we were taken to see the dam wall itself (left). It was overwhelmingly huge and served to remind us again of how small we really are. In some ways it was a bit scary thinking about how much water the reservoir holds and the disaster that would occur if the dam broke. The tour guides reassured us on that point, describing ongoing maintenance and all the high-tech equipment to monitor the dam itself, to make sure its integrity can be maintained. Having admired–and become somewhat bemused by–all the equipment, instrumentation, and the general information about the facility and its construction, we were off to drive across the dam itself.

We exited the bus at the top of the dam and looked out on the reservoir, which is on the same massive scale as the dam itself. The lake stretches back about 200km into the Manicouagan Crater—one of the largest impact craters in the world—and in doing so, has become one of the world's largest reservoirs. This reservoir is also a great fishing location for Atlantic salmon, lake trout and northern pike, something else we hadn't even thought about.

From our viewpoint at the top of the dam we could look down on the road we would have to travel the following day, and we realized that our bus had been traveling, or rather creeping, up that same road! It was not a reassuring feeling, especially after the rough driving we had already experienced. But ever the optimists, we thought if an old school bus could do it, so could we.

The road we would soon travel

Once the tour was over we found our way to the Belvedere. This is a large open area with a number of parking spots, just right for RVs. It is on a hill overlooking the river and the dam, and as we looked at the dam from that vantage point we had a greater impression of the size of it and its relationship to the landscape. That view served to reinforce our understanding of the immensity of the dam and reservoir, and its place in the environment.

As we faced the road the following morning we followed our usual pattern of driving. I usually drive in the morning, while Bob takes the afternoon shift. This has worked well for us over many years of driving and there seems to be no reason to change our well ingrained habits. Beyond Manic 5 the map we got in Baie Comeau indicated we would be traveling on gravel for a significant distance, and provided the gravel was in good condition, we hoped it would be better than the paved road from the previous day. As we left Manic 5 and started climbing the gravel road from the base of the dam we were able to relax as the surface was in good condition. The further we drove the more confidence we gained in our ability to enjoy this experience. So we started to relax and just enjoy the drive. This gravel road was not too busy this early in the morning, and while there were still steep inclines and numerous curves—with signs like 'Bends next 5km'—there were many smooth, straight stretches. The scenery was wonderful, with long vistas on either side of the road, and we were really enjoying the experience. All in all, the first part of the road was quite adequate for a gravel surface. Then, our enjoyment was suddenly brought to an end when we found *washboard*! Initially these sections were fairly short, so while it was not pleasant, we coped and so did the vehicle. Then came the culverts. As before, they were being replaced so there were frequent stops for single lane traffic. Then things changed.

A rushing torrent passing under the road

We came across more washboard, but this time it wasn't just a few hundred metres; it went on and on and didn't stop. The RV rattled and shook, doors and drawers started opening and closing on their own; the chesterfield cushions started exploring the inside of the vehicle, and enjoyed the company of the door well; the bathroom mat vibrated itself to the kitchen area, and the kitchen mat joined the chesterfield cushions. We dreaded to think what was happening in the cupboards and the fridge, but we knew when we stopped we would find out. The washboard surface thankfully gave out after what seemed like kilometres and we both heaved a big sigh of relief. Sadly, this was short lived, because it soon started up again! This time it went on for many more kilometres. Altogether, this stretch of highway lasted for over 100km, and by the end of it I was thinking very unkind thoughts about it. Bob and I had thought the Dempster and the Top of the World highways were bad and difficult, but by the time we eventually found some asphalt we knew that this road was much, much worse. At one point I actually stopped the RV because I thought I heard an unusual noise and was worried about the tires. Fortunately they were fine; it was just the road and vehicle interacting in a weird way. My sympathies lay with the RV! Instead of being a nuisance, the frequent stops for culvert repairs had given me the opportunity to take my hands off the steering wheel and stretch my fingers, which I was beginning to think would be permanently moulded there!

After what seemed to be an eon we drove onto newly paved asphalt. This was a delight, and I could actually drive at the speed limit for a couple of kilometres until we approached one of the few restaurants on the highway. We thankfully stopped for a coffee break and tried to relax before facing the next part of the road. While we were sitting at our table we met a family from Labrador, who were heading home after visiting family in Ontario. They warned us of the next bad patch of gravel, which was about a 100km down the road, but they assured us the rest of the road was adequate. Fortunately they were right about the rest of the road. I drove some of the way, and then Bob took over after lunch, and hit the second stretch of gravel, all 67km of it, plus coping with eleven not very nice rail crossings. Crossing this same train track so many times was really an interesting experience. Naturally there were no warning bells, so as we approached the crossings it was necessary to look both ways to make sure no ore trains were coming! We did encounter one train, and for several of the crossings we found ourselves either ahead of it or behind it, which made crossing the tracks more of a challenge.

This part of the road was extremely unpleasant; more washboard and more vibration. We weaved in and out of the countryside, crossing and re-crossing the train tracks. We thought it might have been easier if our wheels were suitable for railroads, which at least looked straight and level, while the poor road had to curve and bend around marshes, rocky hills and many other nondescript obstacles. We shook and vibrated in sympathy with our poor, abused vehicle as it continued to shake and vibrate its way across this unforgiving road. After what seemed like a millennium we actually found asphalt, and as the road improved somewhat Bob commented, "If this had been one of those machines that vibrate your body to lose weight, we would have lost at least 20 pounds each!"

After the eleventh railroad crossing we approached the town of Fermont

Finally the gravel gave way to paved road at Fermont and the driving conditions were marginally better. Highway 389 becomes Highway 500 at the Labrador border, and from this point to Labrador City it is mainly used by big trucks. Even though it was not in the best condition, it was so much better than the gravel that we didn't really care. Realistically, we knew the highway only existed because of natural resource extraction and hydroelectric generation. Without them it would never have been built. However, having driven this road, and understanding it is the only road into Labrador, we really felt it should be kept in better condition. The people of Labrador need a road to the south, and travelers exploring this beautiful country should at least have access via a road that is reasonable and safe to travel on. Even if it has to be gravel—and that may be necessary—at least there needs to be more maintenance to ensure the safety and comfort of those using it.

When we finally arrived in Labrador City we easily found the welcome centre. Bob looked into finding a campsite for the night, while I chatted with the very friendly ladies in the gift shop. After hearing our tale of the road they were very understanding, and hoped the rest of our visit would be better. One of the ladies felt we needed some extra support and gave us a couple of soft drinks to help us on our way. A very kind, and much appreciated gesture. After buying some postcards for the grandchildren, they sent us on our way in true Labrador fashion: They both came out from behind their counter, cried, "I think you need a big hug!" and did exactly that. What a wonderful welcome to this fascinating part of the world.

After our long and difficult day of driving, we finally arrived at our lakeside campground some 40km east of Labrador City, and were greeted with such warmth that we felt entirely at home and happily settled into our spot. Now we had to check what damage, if any, the poor RV had suffered. Bob was busy connecting the van to the water and hydro hook-ups when he noticed some creamy-coloured slime on the bodywork. It turned out to be dried-up milk! After a few minutes of puzzlement we remembered how, on some of the rougher roads in Quebec a couple of days earlier, one of our bags of milk had sprung a leak in the fridge. Naturally we had cleaned up the fridge and thought that was it was it, but as we looked at the mess on the outside of the vehicle we found that some of the milk had dripped through the drain in the fridge and had emptied onto the outside of the van! This was a new one for us! So, first things first, clean-up time. Then it was supper time and a new surprise. As I opened the food cupboard I found the bottle of olive oil on its side and inevitably spilt everywhere! So started the second clean-up job. Next we went through the fridge and found the items had followed the example of the chesterfield cushions and floor mats, and had rearranged themselves in order to meet new friends inside this rather small space! Therefore, task number three had to be rapidly undertaken before I could even think of making supper! Ah, a relaxing glass of wine would be nice to enjoy while supper was cooking. Oh wait! Our normally well-behaved wine boxes had chosen to migrate towards the other end of the cupboard, but thankfully they had maintained their integrity, which was a blessing. So, having poured a glass of wine, I went to wash my hands in our little bathroom sink prior to cooking, and innocently opened the cupboard get the soap. Now it was the turn of my shampoo to jump out as it tried to wash my hair right then and there! By this time I was not amused, so the shampoo was put firmly back where it belonged and Bob and I finally enjoyed our supper and our relaxing glass of wine. It had been that sort of day.

After supper we took a leisurely walk around the campsite, and the calmness of the lake helped us relax and to really appreciate we were in Labrador, and ready to embrace all it had to offer. Later on that evening we spent some time talking to the owner of the campsite and with her help we were able to book a tour of the Churchill Falls Hydroelectric Facility for the next day, and also to book our next campsite in Happy Valley-Goose Bay. The warmth of the people we had met more than made up for the tough driving, and by the end of the day we were feeling much better and were looking forward to seeing what the morrow would bring.

A peaceful end after a long day

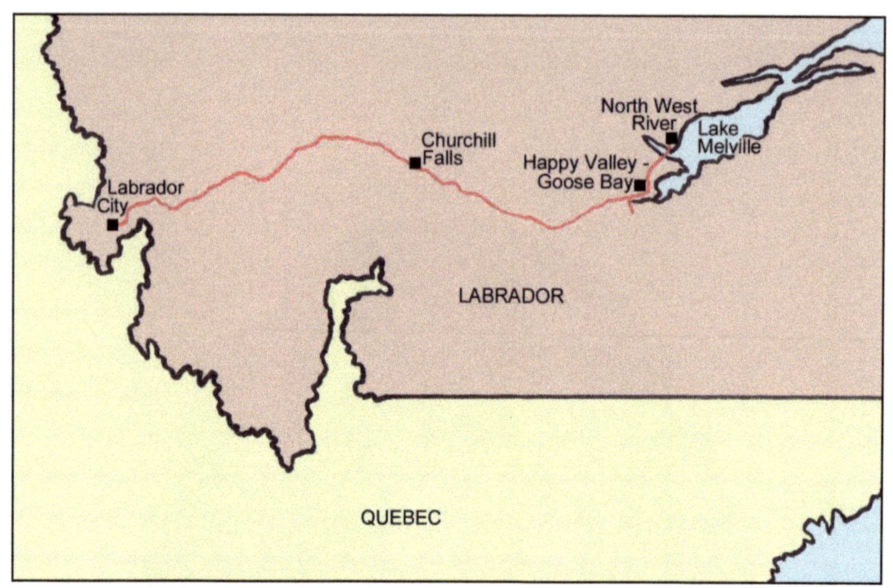

Labrador City to Happy Valley-Goose Bay	541km
TOTAL	541km

Chapter Three
Labrador City to Happy Valley-Goose Bay

Waking up the next morning was a rewarding experience because now we were finally in Labrador and heading towards Happy Valley-Goose Bay. We were in a new and very unfamiliar part of Canada. Once our friendly campground owner had confirmed our tour of the Churchill Falls hydroelectric facility, we were on our way. The road was a joy, smoothly paved with no potholes or gravel; such a pleasant change from the previous two days of driving. It was time to relax and enjoy a very different landscape.

In all our travels we have enjoyed and appreciated the changing landscapes, whether it is driving through the tundra in the north, or the tropical and sub-tropical vegetation in the south. So as we headed east we observed how much the landscape was changing; the trees, black spruce mainly, were shorter and not as densely spaced as those seen further south. There was much more muskeg and any number of small lakes and ponds scattered across the landscape. Rivers and streams kept showing up, and as we crossed them we figured they must all join the Churchill River at some point downstream.

One of the many streams we crossed in this barren place

We had left the campsite quite early in the day, and a few hours along we came across a small truck pulled over to the side. I was driving and took care to pass it safely, but Bob noticed what looked like a moose or a caribou in the vegetation near the road. This was exciting; our first big wildlife spotting of this trip. Naturally, we stopped and made our way back to the parked truck, and immediately understood why the truck had stopped. There before us was a full-grown caribou, as his huge rack of antlers showed. A really wonderful sight. We stayed and watched for several minutes as it wandered about grazing on the vegetation, while we chatted to the couple from the other vehicle. There was no evidence of the rest of the herd, which made us all wonder why this splendid animal was off by itself. After the caribou wandered of we got back on the road once more, hoping to see other wonderful sights. This was one of those occasions when my camera was no real use. The animal was too far away for the amateur photographer that I am. Bob and I just remember the gloriousness of the animal, and hope one day to see another such specimen.

Churchill Falls is a small town in the middle of nowhere, and just about halfway between Labrador City and Happy Valley-Goose Bay. Its claim to fame is the huge hydroelectric station. So once we arrived there we were interested to learn more about the place, and what it must be like to live there year round. As always on these long drives, we fill up with gas whenever we can find it. We soon learned that the local gas station was the only one for over 250km in either direction, so it was very important to feed our always thirsty vehicle, and not risk running out of fuel before making it to Happy Valley-Goose Bay! Following the directions from the gas station staff, we found our way to the Town Hall, where we confirmed out reservations for the tour and also found out that we were to meet our tour guide at the shopping mall.

This shopping mall is the 'Everything Place' of Churchill Falls. The school, the restaurants, the hotel, stores, library and post office are all found in this one building, which makes it very convenient for the residents. We found the local restaurant and had a very enjoyable lunch there. The other major advantage of this spot was the access to WiFi, so while we waited for our lunch, Bob and I were able to check our emails. Now, after this experience, I really can't criticize others who do the same thing! After lunch it was time to meet our tour guide.

Our tour guide, Paula, was a very friendly local woman who had been brought up in Churchill Falls. As an adult she had moved away to Halifax where she lived for many years with her husband and children. Her husband had fallen in love with Churchill Falls and after his retirement they moved back here, initially for a brief time but which has now been extended over several years. He works at the power plant, while Paula has held several part-time jobs, including acting as a tour guide for the hydroelectric station. They are both very content to be living here and have no plans to move back to the south in the near future.

We were very curious about life in this area, and especially how the locals coped with the winter. To start with, snowfall is extreme by Ottawa standards and the temperatures in the winter are ridiculously low -40 to -50°C at times in January. The children are all bused to school, but in the winter the younger kids have time off when it gets to around -40°C, while the older kids have to wait until it is colder than that! It did not sound very pleasant at all, and such statistics made us happy to be living in Ottawa, where the extremes are not as quite great.

We were driven to the hydroelectric site by van, and after clearing security we were outfitted with safety vest, hard hat and earplugs. Then, with all our gear on, we rode an elevator deep down into the working part of the facility. Paula described the building of the dam and how the working areas of the generating station had been created in the granite formation surrounding it.

Deep underground, the entire facility is carved out of ancient rock

The rock had been gradually carved away to form tunnels and bays throughout the area to provide space for all the equipment needed to produce electricity. This was a huge surprise to us, and we had never really thought about how the whole facility had been constructed. We had assumed the construction followed others we had seen or read about. Here, the juxtaposition of the modern machinery on one side with the ancient granite rock, merely half a billion years old was quite a contrast.

The huge transformers and other heavy equipment needed for the working of the plant had to be shipped by rail to Labrador City, and then transported by road on a huge vehicle designed for this purpose. The top and only speed of the vehicle was 5km per hour. And while it was traveling no other vehicles could use the road because it took up the entire width! This was the same road we had been driving since leaving Labrador City, the only difference was that it was now paved. This was also a reminder that most of the roads in this area are more about the need for industrial transportation than tourist travel, something we tend to forget when traveling. Other equipment, somewhat smaller in scale, was brought to the site and assembled there.

One of the generators with the panels removed for servicing, showing the rotor in the centre and the stator coils around the outside

As we continued the tour, passing through huge manmade corridors connecting the various areas, it felt a bit like our walking tours of the naturally-formed Mammoth Cave tunnels in Kentucky, which were on the same enormous scale. We were shown the emergency refuge areas, which could be sealed quickly against flooding. They have never needed to be used but it was still it a reminder of the potential risks posed by these massive projects. There are plans to create more dams downstream to allow the water to be reused, and thus create more electricity for use in Labrador and the Maritime Provinces. While we were touring the facility, Paula shared many anecdotes about the project and the people involved with it, which made our tour so much more enjoyable. At the same time, we came away in awe of the work done to create this enormous facility. It was a very thought provoking experience.

After our tour we headed east again toward our destination for the night, Happy Valley-Goose Bay. We had enjoyed wonderful road conditions driving to Churchill Falls, and were a little concerned about the long stretch of gravel that awaited us before we reached our destination. When we had expressed our concerns, we had been assured the road was 'not that bad', and had recently been re-graded, which was reassuring to hear. So we actually believed that this particular piece of road, while it might be slow, would not be as bad as some we had seen. Our campsite was booked and the owner/manager just told us that if we got in late to find a spot and hook up for the night, so we had no concern about that.

We had the same beautiful conditions on starting that we had experienced in the morning, so much reassured we made good time. We cheerfully thought we would be in Happy Valley-Goose Bay in time for an early supper. How nice was that? Then came the gravel section! Once again a washboard surface showed itself in all its horror. We hoped it would just be for a short distance, but it wasn't! The re-graded road had also been re-graveled, so the fresh gravel was spraying up everywhere; the large clouds of dust created by us and other drivers made seeing the road at times quite difficult; the potholes showed their sad little faces and tried to capture our wheels; and the vibration in the vehicle and throughout our bodies was horrendous. This had now become the new normal; everything inside the vehicle started moving again, and those cupboard doors and drawers, already bungeed closed, started up making their own music with a chorus of bangs and rattles as they tried to open and close on their own! Of good smooth driving there was little, and as soon as there was any relief and we relaxed slightly the road would deteriorate once more. This wonderful experience lasted for much of the 65km piece of gravel road. We really booted it along and at top speed of 40km/h, or less.

Another roadworks encounter. It is gratifying to know that regular work is being done to at least maintain the conditions

Our idea of a leisurely early supper faded away with each kilometre we drove. Once this section of the road was done, though, we were back on asphalt and suddenly the driving became much easier and more manageable. As we drove into Happy Valley-Goose Bay we resolved to give ourselves and our hardworking van a rest, and rent a car for the couple of days we were there. We found our resting place for the night, and after being greeted kindly by the campsite owners we were able to stop and relax.

We woke up the next morning much refreshed, partly because we were actually here in Goose Bay with time to explore the area before our voyage, but also because our blackout curtains, originally created for our trip to Inuvik in 2012 (see *Points North and West*), helped us to a good night's sleep. Labrador is much further north than Ottawa, which meant the nights were noticeably shorter and lighter, so reducing the level of light during the late evening and early morning hours really helped us both.

Our first task was to pick up our rental car at the airport, and our very kind campsite owner drove us to the airport. We had to pass through the Canadian Forces Base to get to the airport, which was a bit of a surprise, but it really did make sense; the Forces were there first. After picking up the car we drove slowly through the area and Bob noticed a Catalina, one of the old flying boats, proudly 'flying' on a pedestal in the base. We stopped to look at it and imagine all the places it had been and the things the crew might have seen. It was symbolic of a long past era of flight.

A venerable Catalina flying boat

Now, driving a small car we were footloose and fancy free, and headed directly to the tourist information centre in town. This was not on the scale we had expected; just a small room in one of the many equally small buildings in a small town. We were really excited to learn about the Beach Days, an annual celebration held at North West River, a small town about 30km north of our campsite. It sounded like a lot of fun so once our chores were done we packed a picnic lunch and made our way to there to enjoy all the festivities.

We had been told about a local waterfall that was a short walk from the only road going to North West River, and we thought would make a peaceful diversion on the way to North West River and the festivities it had to offer. We passed right by the signpost without seeing it, so we decided to drive on and maybe do this walk later. It was a good thing we were not driving the RV; North West River was packed with cars parked in every available spot close to the festival site. We added our little rental to the rest and wandered around this charming little village.

We could hear the band from a quite a distance, and by following the music we found the beach and the stage where the party was in full swing. After a brief walk around the site we found ourselves at one of the tables in the central grassy area, and began a conversation with a young couple presently living here. She was originally from Alberta while he hailed from Idaho, where they had met when she was attending school. They were avid cyclists and had been married in New York City after cycling there from Idaho on a fundraising drive. As we listened to their tale of their courtship, we both thought that having survived such a trip their relationship must be very strong, and this boded well for the longevity of their marriage. They left New York to cycle up to Newfoundland and have lived here ever since. At present she is employed while he waits for his permanent residency papers, a very familiar story. This has been a long process for them as he is not permitted to work until his residency is confirmed, which makes life somewhat of a challenge for them. We commiserated with them, and wished them well for the future. After this lovely lunchtime interlude we set out to explore North West River again.

General view of the Beach Days picnic area

When we first arrived in North West River we had no idea of the history of this pretty place, but visits to museums and craft stores (described a little later) soon filled in the picture. Apparently, the first settlement here was over 250 years ago, when in 1743 a French fur trapper set up a year-round trading post. Later on the English navy arrived and exploited the very plentiful salmon and cod to feed the ships' crews. The official settlement occurred in 1785, the population increased with the European influx in 1835, and of course the Hudson's Bay Company opened a store in 1836. In its characteristic predatory fashion it soon bought out the fur traders and created a monopoly! The trading posts expanded over the following years and farming became part of the landscape, with those sturdy plants and animals that could flourish in the climate of the area. By the late 19th and early 20th centuries there was much exploration and mapping, all starting from North West River.

Although we didn't realize it at the time, Dr Wilfred Grenfell had played an important part in the healthcare of this region of Labrador, setting up nursing stations, hospitals and schools all along the coast. One of the hospitals was built in North West River and operated for many years. This hospital, together with the Hudson's Bay Company store and a residential school allowed this charming place to become a thriving community. Once the Canadian Forces airbase was established in Goose Bay it became the economic hub of central Labrador, and so North West River was relegated to being a small town with a fascinating history.

After our brief stop at the beach we drove to the north end of the town to visit the Labrador Interpretation Centre. The docent at the front desk had spent some time in Ottawa, so after a brief chat to share experiences, she gave us a brief guided tour and then left us alone to wander around the Centre. The exhibition was really well done and explored the history of Labrador in sequential displays. These described the four groups of people who now comprise the population of Labrador: the Innu, the Inuit, the Metis and the Settlers. The displays took us through the history of all these groups and helped us understand how they lived and worked, in their own communities and cooperatively. It was good to realize how much was shared and how these diverse people had blended together and learned from one another.

Very close to the locale of the Beach Festival we found a charming Arts and Craft store. In one corner a desk set up with a pile of books so, of necessity (because who are *we* to ignore books of any sort?) we approached the lady at the desk. Her name was Anne Budgell and she was launching her book, *Dear Everybody* (see Resources, p. 274), a biography about a family friend who had lived in North West River, and had spent some years on the trap-lines with her trapper husband. Barbara Mundy Groves was a New York socialite who had come to Labrador to work with the Grenfell Mission and had fallen in love with Labrador and its people. The story sounded fascinating, so we bought a copy and enjoyed reading it, learning even more about life on the trap-line in the winter, as well as the work of Dr Grenfell and his mission. Our curiosity about this man and his work was finally assuaged almost two weeks later in St Anthony, when we visited the Grenfell Mission.

The Museum, which we explored next, was laid out as a Hudson's Bay Store from the late 19th century. There was a wonderful exhibit of living on the trap-line, which included a model of a tilt, the little huts built by the trappers for survival in the long, harsh winter. The tilt we examined was very small, and made us wonder how anyone could live in it. I have slept in small two-person tents that were bigger than that! We later learned that a tilt of this size was likely only used for a quick overnight stay, and that the 'base camp tilts' would be much bigger, which to my mind was a good thing. As we continued to explore this little museum we came across some wonderful working models demonstrating the many of the activities of the area. They comprised little vignettes of life, dating from the present to well over a century ago; from stores to houses to fishing areas to early radio or Marconi stations. Dr Grenfell was well represented in these displays as well, and the models of his hospital ships were beautiful.

The excellent exhibit of early medical tools was both interesting and amusing. So many of those implements were very similar to those we use today. Granted the more modern equipment has been somewhat refined, but when in desperate circumstances these instruments could likely be brought back into service after a good cleaning. The descriptive panels dealt with the doctors practicing in the region over the last hundred years. It was somewhat scary to think that the only medical support available in most of the remote communities was by dogsled in the winter and hospital ship in the summer. It made us thankful we are living in a city where all such supports are close by.

Before we left the museum we had a talk with to the two young ladies working there. They were Inuit and were happy to talk about the distinction between Innu and Inuit. The Innu in this area are Naskapi, Montagnais and Cree, while the Inuit are from northern Labrador. We chatted for quite a while, and during the course of our discussion they eagerly shared their knowledge about the history of the exhibits. This led to a discussion on the lost skills of most cultures today, and the need to encourage the younger generation to learn about and practice those skills. They showed such pride in their culture, while lamenting the loss of skills, and spoke about efforts to learn these skills from the elders of the community.

The inlet beyond North West River, leading into Lake Melville

It was the end of a long day and time to start back to the campsite. As we walked back to the car—shoe-horned into yet another tiny parking spot—we had fun watching the finish of a canoe race. This was an important part of the activities of Beach Days, and we enjoyed the support of the crowd as they cheered on the participants. As we drove back to our campsite we spotted the signpost for the waterfall, and so planned to take the time to explore it on the following day.

We were intrigued by a rig parked next to us in the campsite; a Toyota Land Cruiser with a variety of adaptations. The couple who owned it were from Holland and had designed and built many of the upgrades. Over the last several years this very adventurous couple had taken their rig through Africa, Australia, the Middle East and South America. Now they were exploring North America, having visited Inuvik in 2013. We chatted about our experiences in 2012 when we were in Inuvik and Alaska, and found their stories very similar. As we went back to our modest rig for supper we wondered where else this couple would go, and what else they would see. The idea of having no permanent home to return to simply had no appeal for us. Travel is wonderful, but so is coming home.

As always on our trips, we needed to take time for mundane tasks, and this often leads to interesting discussions with area residents. This trip was no different and while I sat in the Laundromat, catching up with emails, I was easily distracted by another client, a friendly lady from the area. It was this lovely lady who first told me about cloudberries, otherwise known as Labrador bakeapples. She said they were now coming into season, and once I told her we planned to travel down to Red Bay about two weeks hence, she suggested we stop and pick some en route. Her instructions were clear and basic. Look for people in the marshy areas beside the road carrying buckets; they would be the ones picking the fruit, so just park the vehicle and join them. It sounded enjoyable so I assured her we would stop if we spotted pickers. She was also a mine of information about the gravel highway to Red Bay, and she was under the impression it would not be an issue for us in the RV. We were somewhat skeptical, but hoped she was right. However, after our previous experiences…

I also told her of our planned trip up the coast to Nain and learned, much to my surprise, that the ship had only just started its regular run. Apparently, the vessel needed a number of repairs and had been delayed starting its regular schedule this season. The wonderful part of her information was her conviction that we would see both icebergs and whales, attractions we had really been hoping for.

After our chores that day we spent another happy afternoon in North West River. On the way we took the short nature walk that we had missed the day before. It was a pleasant little walk up a small hill, ending at the base of a pretty little waterfall (left). And then it was off to the Festival once more. We enjoyed the music provided by a range of local musicians and took great pleasure in watching the crowd, especially when they would begin jigging to the music.

After a while we stopped at the tent of an Innu elder who was making Indian doughnuts, so naturally we had to try one. It was not as sweet as most commercially produced ones, which made a pleasant change, and we both enjoyed sharing it. The best part was peering through the flap into her tent and watching her cooking. The tent was incredibly hot inside, and we watched as she formed the doughnuts on a sheet of steel and cooked them in oil in a large skillet over a wood stove. The stovepipe vented out of the top of the tent. The tent contained everything she needed for the task at hand, and with the pine fronds on the floor it appeared very homely and comfortable. Her baking really could not have been any fresher.

Making doughnuts the traditional way

We left with our doughnut in hand and just wandered around again, enjoying the ambience, and spending a time-out by people-watching. It was a beautiful day, and it was obvious the whole community was out there enjoying the experience and the weather. At one point the show's emcee announced a competition for the most polished motorbike; the winner would be chosen by ballot through the peoples' choice. Bob could not miss this, so we went to check them all. There were about 15 bikes, all looking like new, highly polished and immaculately turned out. At the very end of the line was a very ordinary pedal bike with a competition number on it, which amused us. Since the winner was to be decided by the people's choice, I chose this pedal bike along with my other choices. After all, somebody had to support it! Bob chose a gorgeous Indian, a rare machine and the only one in the show. After we had made our choices it was back to sit in the sun in front of the stage, watching performers and listening to music. After some time, and many more announcements about the need for people to come forward and vote for the bikes, the winner was announced. It was not one of the ones we had chosen, but the winner was quite the beautiful machine. After listening to more music, we realized we needed to get back to the campsite and get ourselves organized for the next, and in some ways, perhaps the most anticipated part of the this trip.

Back at the campsite, we noticed a couple from Arizona sitting in the shade, so we spent some time talking to them. They had encountered difficulties driving here with their trailer, and their experiences helped us appreciate how lucky we had been driving over rough roads with virtually no damage. Like us, they had driven up from Baie Comeau, but as they neared the end of the highway a leaf spring had broken on their trailer. They were stuck on the side of the road for quite some time while they tried to locate a tow truck. It was a bit of a wake-up call for us, as they had discovered the hard way that service calls may not be answered quickly, and that tow trucks cannot be assumed to be easily available. They never did get a tow truck, but they were able to limp into Labrador City at the remarkable speed of 5kph, with the help from another driver and a log of wood jammed between the axle and the undercarriage. They were very grateful for the support of this other traveler, who had followed them with his four-way flashers going, helped them to park, and then assisted in getting their trailer fixed.

They spoke warmly of him and of the hospitality they found when they finally arrived in Labrador City.

Later we chatted to our newly arrived neighbours in a camper van from Ontario. They were from the Niagara region, and like us they intended to take the coastal ship up to Nain before continuing down to Newfoundland and the other Maritime provinces. We compared notes on the state of the roads and concluded that when we returned from Nain it would be wise to travel in convoy, just in case mechanical issues showed up. They told us that the Newfoundland and Labrador government offered a free satellite phone borrowing scheme, although they had been unable to acquire one. It said something for the state of the roads that the government considered this a good idea!

And now, for the first time since we had left home, Bob was able to practice his trumpet. He had brought it with him, and had turned a wooden mute on the lathe so he could practice relatively quietly during our adventures. This proved to be one of the few occasions when this was possible. It made, however, a fitting fanfare to the first part of our trip.

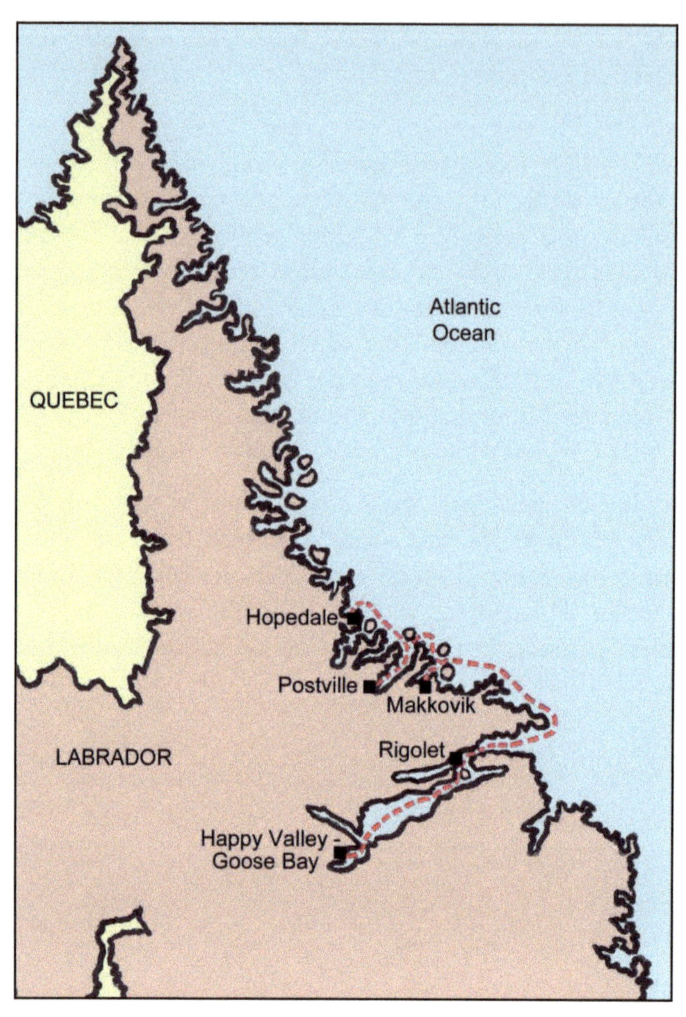

Goose Bay to Rigolet	86nm
Rigolet to Makkovik	147nm
Makkovik to Postville	40nm
Postville to Hopedale	62nm
TOTAL	335km

(Statistics courtesy of Nunatsiavut Marine)

Chapter Four
Happy Valley-Goose Bay to Hopedale

Finally, the time had arrived for our much anticipated voyage to Nain, the furthest point north we would be able to travel on this trip. There are very few ways of getting to Nain even in summer, the only viable options for tourists in particular are by the ship we were booked on, or by light aircraft. For the local population, off-road vehicles might be used for short trips during the summer, and those with access to small boats or canoes use them to travel between the villages. However, the ship is the principle means of travel up the coast in summer, especially for the larger items of freight. In the winter the sea is frozen up some distance out, so supply ships are unable to service the coastal villages. The only options are skidoos or light aircraft, which make the habitations slightly more accessible. This reality was brought home to us during our time on the ship.

The MV Northern Ranger

We returned our rental car, parked the RV in the storage area of the Marine Terminal, and prepared ourselves for a week of very new experiences. While waiting for our tickets at the Nunatsiavut Marine terminal the reality of life along this shoreline was emphasized to us; the line-up was long and slow, and as we looked around we realized what a varied group our fellow passengers would be. There were the obviously tourists; there were family groups from grandparents to babies; students returning home from school; a group of women who had been shopping in Happy Valley-Goose Bay; and many, many others. We were relieved we had pre-booked our cabin, because it became clear as we waited, that others in line would have liked to have done so too. This first look at our voyage of discovery really reinforced the message that this ship is like a regular 'bus service', allowing the people regular access to each other up and down the coast. The MV *Northern Ranger*, to be our residence for the next five days, was a mixed passenger and freight vessel on its regular run.

Our baggage was loaded into a side door at dockside, and then we climbed the gangplank to the upper deck, and went in search of our cabin. Our little cabin was the basic model, with four bunks and a small washroom but no shower. The communal showers were close by, so that wasn't an issue. The next level of cabin 'luxury' did include shower facilities, which would have been nice, but hardly a necessity. Once we had made ourselves at home, we started to explore more of the ship. It was not a very big vessel; only four decks, which comprised a large lounge, a cafeteria, and two decks of cabins. The rest of the ship was occupied by engine rooms, holds fore and aft, crew quarters, and all the other functioning parts of the vessel, so it didn't take too long to find our way about.

The lounge seemed to be the most popular place. It was a large area with two television screens, lots of comfortable seating, a computer (though we never found out if it really worked) and several tables with upright chairs. It was packed with the many families traveling up the coast, and to our surprise we recognized several people we had seen at the North West River Beach Festival. This underscored how important this service was; it appeared many people had come down for the festival, had met friends and family, and had also caught up with their shopping, resupplying their own households with much needed things. Piles of bags and packages were everywhere. Many of these families had already staked out claims to various areas in the lounge, and were settled in for the long haul home, whether it would be the first port of call at Rigolet, or the last stop in Nain.

Returning on deck, we went aft and watched the wharf-side and deck crew loading the hold. To judge by the variety of goods being loaded, and seeing the demand for this trip, we could imagine the impact on the community of the late start to the shipping season. As we later learned, there was also a purely cargo ship servicing these communities on a regular run, so while cargo could be transported to the villages up and down the coast, there was no practical way for the people to travel out to see friends or even just to get household supplies.

Supplies of all sorts being loaded at the dockside

Looking around this little floating community, it was clear that all the various ethnicities of the locale were fully represented: Innu, Inuit, Metis and Caucasian, as well as people from other backgrounds who made these tiny villages their homes. And the children! Over the last several years there have been many media reports indicating that the fastest-growing population in Canada is found in the native communities, and we could certainly see that here. There were quite a few very young children, in many cases with very young looking mothers, while in the larger families the children, whether they were siblings or cousins, spanned the age range from babies to pre-teens and older. However, it became very clear that this was a close-knit community, and that most of the passengers either knew or were related to each other, and this gave the voyage the feel of one large communal party. There was one very pregnant mother with a small toddler in hand and we wondered how she would cope, but then we saw that the grandmother was along as well, and helping her with the little one. And when grandmother was too busy, or had had enough, others in the group stepped in. One large family gathering occupied a group of chairs facing each other, and had set up their own little private space. The children were everywhere, running around, laughing, shouting and generally having fun. They were happy to be entertained by any adult or older child and by each other, although at times observing through our citified eyes, there seemed to be very little supervision. One young girl, aged around 10, trotted round the centre of the salon, and just for fun Bob began counting her circuits and indicating them to her with raised fingers. She made 77 circuits and we figured she was going to sleep well that night!

Everyone had food of some sort, and before the ship even left Goose Bay many of the families were sitting down and enjoying the lunches they had prepared for the trip. Others waited until the cafeteria was open, and enjoyed the ham and fries or mashed potato, or perhaps the hamburger, chicken nuggets and poutine options. We also joined them in the cafeteria that first morning, but not being fans of fast food we brought own lunch with us, although to justify our being there we bought tea and coffee as 'rent' for the table. The cafeteria had very strict opening hours: one hour each for breakfast, lunch and supper.

While we were eating we met our acquaintances from the campsite in Happy Valley-Goose Bay. Michael and Linda had recently retired and were seeing the country in the same way we were. Like us, they found the food in the cafeteria not really to their liking but made the best of it, and quickly found out that if they asked for something a little different, their wishes would be accommodated by the thoughtful kitchen crew. As we soon learned, this small cafeteria caters more to the regular passengers traveling this route than those of us who are using it as a tourist attraction. This was obviously a working ship and everything about it indicated that. Even so, it was comfortable in a workman like way, and the crew were all very helpful and willing to make the trip as pleasant as possible.

This was certainly an interesting ship on which to be passengers. At one point we went onto the deck to watch the scenery drift by, and hopefully see some icebergs, and naturally started talking with two couples from Newfoundland. The ladies were sisters and were visiting the places where their late father had lived and worked. Apparently, he had not talked much about his past experiences, and now he was gone they wanted to learn more about what his life may have looked like so many years ago. Later in the day I sat next to a lady from Postville, one of the small villages we would be visiting. She seemed to know many of the families aboard. I was interested in her thoughts about the children in particular, but their parents as well, and as we chatted I learned that she was a teacher in the Postville School. No wonder she knew so many people on the ship; she had taught so many of them. She was very happy to talk about both the joys and the challenges of working in this area. She was originally from the Goose Bay area, but had been living and working in Postville for many years. Her children were now grown and had moved away for work and further education, but she was very happy teaching the next generation of children, and at this point was happy to stay in the area.

The intricately carved coastline offered gorgeous seascapes

It was now time for supper on our first day aboard, so we went down to see what was on offer. Like so many of the passengers, we had brought some supplies on board, specifically for our breakfasts and lunches. But for supper we needed to see what the cafeteria had to offer for our first proper meal on the ship. The place was crowded and there was nowhere to sit, so we chose take our spaghetti—with much less pasta than usually provided—and garlic toast, to enjoy with a glass of wine, back in the privacy of our cabin. The ship was 'dry' so officially we were not allowed to bring any alcohol on board, which we hadn't realized when we boarded. So we were very discrete when enjoying the occasional glass of wine.

The first stop of the voyage was at Rigolet, only about six and a half hours after leaving Happy Valley-Goose Bay. The friendly teacher, whose name I never learned, told me that most of the people on the ship were from Rigolet and would disembark there, and that only a few passengers would board. Things would therefore start to quieten down a little, especially in the lounge area. She was right; the salon was almost empty after that brief stop. Looking down on the dock from the ship's deck we saw it was crowded with people, and as passengers walked down the gangplank they were greeted by family members; children running towards parents, grandparents greeting grandchildren, a whole family and community welcome to those who had been away for just a few days. It was lovely to watch this warm recognition for those who had been absent. We encountered this show of affection time and time again as we stopped at all the little ports up and down the coast.

At every port of call there would be crowds meeting the ship

We were allowed to disembark for a brief while, so we wandered into the craft store and picked up a couple of postcards for the family. This was a craft store like no other. It was very small, and in many way poorly appointed, with rough tables and shelves around the walls. There was one place that appeared to be a craft work area, but while we were there it was not in use, perhaps because it was late in the evening and the store had only opened because the ship had come in. The quality of the crafts was excellent and the prices good. We found some lovely earrings made of sealskin, as well as sealskin mitts and slippers. I was very tempted by them, but did not buy. There were rolls of cured seal skin for sale too, which was incredibly soft. I would have loved that, but what to make with it? I made a comment about the yarn on display at the back of the store, and one of the passengers from Makkovik suggested I wait until we arrived there the next day, since there was a bigger craft store there.

Our evening's entertainment out in the Rigolet inlet

At that point there was a cry of "Whale!" so Bob and I rushed off to the water's edge, where a fin whale was calmly swimming and feeding on capelin, or so we were told, right there in the inlet of Rigolet. We were both so excited and totally mesmerized by the whale, and spent quite some time taking pictures of this amazing animal. I was able to get a couple of reasonable but not great shots while just enjoying watching its antics. This was a perfect end to a very busy day, so once we were back on board it was time to settle down for the night and reminisce about all we had seen. As Rigolet was left behind us we settled down for our first night at sea, finding the gentle rolling motion quite relaxing and conducive to sleep.

Rigolet dwindles in the evening light

Even with all the excitement of the day before, we woke early and made our breakfast in our cabin. It was about then that I realized my packing for this trip was not as thorough as it could have been. By some unfortunate accident all my underwear was back in Happy Valley-Goose Bay, and most definitely not available to me on the ship! Oh well! In the larger scheme of things it was just a minor detail, and it only meant I needed to do laundry every evening, unless of course I could buy underwear in one of the local stores, which was my fallback plan.

Makkovik was the next of our several stops on our way up to Nain. We docked at around 8:00am. Remembering the comment about the craft store, we disembarked and rambled around this pretty place until we found the craft shop. This was much more like the craft shops I had visited in other places; many more good quality craft supplies, some knickknacks to buy, and a very helpful person at the desk. With her help I found some nice yarn and the right size needles suitable for making a pair of socks. Our daughter-in-law in Kingston was the happy recipient of that particular project.

Makkovik from the deck of the ship

Bob and I went back to the ship with both the craft supplies and a number of blackfly bites. Before we had started on our travels we had been warned about the local wildlife—mosquitoes, blackfly, and other biting insects—and now they had found us! It was our first true encounter with these nasty little beasts here in Labrador, and it was not too pleasant. Still, back on board the numbers decreased, which gave us the opportunity to watch the crew unload the cargo. Talk about a mixed bag! We were amazed at the variety of things being unloaded, from an electric fireplace to pallets of eggs, a skid of chilled food, insulation, a plate glass window, and so on. Who thinks about how eggs or frozen food get to the store? We just take it for granted in the city. But here the delivery can only be by ship, and this is totally dependent on the weather and the cooperation of the sea.

Once everything was unloaded onto the dock by the on-board derrick, the crew started to load the cargo that was going further up the coast. As the pallets of frozen crab were being stashed away in the deep freeze, the ladies from Newfoundland, who were also watching, started a discussion of the merits of crab versus lobster (they preferred crab), the difference between Newfoundland lobster and those from Nova Scotia (naturally, in their view Newfoundland lobster was best) and finally the contrast between cold- and warm-water lobster. Given their previous comments, it was to be expected that cold water lobster was by far the superior item. To one who doesn't like lobster, it was quite the amusing conversation.

The ship's horn always sounds several times just before it is due to leave dock, to remind all passengers and guests the ship is pulling away. So, either return on board if you are a passenger, or disembark if you are a guest. Once everybody was on board the gang plank was pulled up, and the ship starting to slowly draw away from the dock. Suddenly, somebody came running up and frantically waving and yelling for the crew to wait! The engines slowed and reversed, the ship pulled back into the dock and waited for the final passengers, who arrived at high speed on a very loaded four-wheeler. Of the two adults and three children piled on the back of the vehicle, the mother and two of the children came on board. They had been visiting the grandparents for a little while and were now returning home. No doubt the children would have liked a longer visit, and they nearly got one! This was another example to us of the 'family' nature of the ship; the captain had halted the progress of this huge vessel at the expense of his timetable, just so a family would not be inconvenienced.

The route from Makkovik to Postville took us a little further out to sea, giving us hope we would see an iceberg or two. We had heard from another passenger that he had spotted icebergs very early in the morning, just before we had docked in Makkovik. His descriptions of the bergs he had seen made us wish we had been up earlier that morning. Just as we were bemoaning our sleeping habits, we spotted an iceberg a long way ahead. We stood outside on the deck and watched it as the ship approached it. We were traveling on a slightly different heading so we didn't get really close to the berg, but just seeing our first iceberg was an amazing feeling. The cameras were out, and I did manage to take a number of pictures of it. We could just about see a second iceberg even further away, which added to the excitement, and we hoped to see some more of them during our voyage. We had been promised icebergs and whales, and now we had seen them both. Amazing!

Our first iceberg, far out to sea

On our arrival in Postville we found our way to the local 'everything store.' Maybe they would stock underwear? The black fly were out in full force and reminded us we were fresh food for them. Next time I will make sure to have the bug spray primed and ready to go! However, feeding the local bug population seemed a small price to pay if I could find new underwear. We walked up the hill to the store and had great fun looking around it. It really was an 'everything store'; food, frozen meats of every description, some rather old and tired fruits and veggies (no doubt they were waiting for another shipment) paints in a limited range of colours, hardware supplies including stovepipes, some garden supplies, all kinds of celebration cards, the usual canned goods, chips, etc., dried goods, boots, towels, paper products and many other items, including a small variety of clothing. But sadly, no underwear in sight! There were several empty shelves while on the full ones things were juxtaposed in a variety of odd ways. I am not sure why the two pairs of jeans lay on the counter with the lacy tablecloths, or the vases sat next to the cleaning items. Did they need a couple of dozen shower curtains, and only three packs of pillow cases? Who knows? There must have been a reason, but I couldn't work it out.

When we disembarked to check out Postville, we had had no opportunity to say goodbye to our friendly teacher. So when we met her driving towards the dock just as we were leaving the store, we were happy to have the opportunity to say goodbye, and to wish her well since the time we had spent with her was so pleasant. She drove us back to the ship and as we chatted it was clear she was happy to be home once more.

The fishing harbour at Postville

Now the ship headed further north to Hopedale, but on this leg of the voyage there was no looking for icebergs; it was cold and rainy and there was very little visibility. It was time for me to enjoy sitting in the salon and to start knitting the latest pair of socks. We were due to arrive in Hopedale at about 5:30 in the afternoon, so along with the rest of the passengers we had an early supper in the cafeteria just prior to docking. We had finally noticed that the opening of the cafeteria changed hour by hour according to the ship's schedule. So supper today was early; maybe tomorrow it would be late, or perhaps on time. It all made perfect sense once we understood the schedule, and were aware of the opening times.

Hopedale was one of those places Bob had really wanted to visit. He has long been interested in the making and playing of brass instruments, and had heard of the influence of the Moravian missionaries, who first arrived in this area in the 1750s, bringing their Christian message along with a brass band tradition. Of all the strangest places for brass playing to take root, this was surely the strangest. Bob was aware of the work of a colleague, hailing from North Carolina, who had studied this brass band movement, and was curious to see what displays the museum would offer.

As we stood on the dock wondering how long it would take us to walk right around the other side of the inlet to the Moravian Mission buildings, a local man appeared at the dock with his pickup truck. This gentleman had come here many years ago, married a girl from the area, and had settled down as the local school teacher. Now, having retired, he was volunteering, giving tourists free tours of the community because he believed it was important for them to see and learn as much as possible about the history of the area. We promptly jumped into his truck, along with several other passengers from the *Northern Ranger*. This was most fortunate since Hopedale is a much larger community that we realized, and without his help it was likely we would have seen very little of this attractive place, and most probably would have never made it to the museum.

We climbed into the truck and got the last two seats. The two couples from Newfoundland were also looking for a ride, so they cheerfully piled into the open back and we all drove off to the Moravian Mission buildings. Our first stop was the museum, located in an 18th century building beside the church. It was beautifully laid out, with very informative panels and many interesting displays. Being the professional he is, Bob spent some time chatting with the curator about the collection, while the rest of us explored the exhibits.

Some of the musical instruments on display. On the wall is a picture of the Inuit brass band

The musical instruments on display held Bob's interest for quite some time, as he looked them over with an experienced eye. I enjoyed wandering around and trying to take in all that I could see.

In the upstairs displays there was a very old and solid woodwork bench, which Bob spent quite some time examining while wishing he could bring it home with us.

Imagine all the work that must have been done at this bench over the years. It carried all the marks of a long and productive working life

The Hopedale Mission and the Moravian church

Right next to the museum was the little church dating from the same period. The community still uses this lovely space, although like so many churches today, the congregation is much smaller. The original organ, dating back to the 1790s started its life in Nain, and then when that one was replaced in the 1820s it was installed in this small church in Hopedale. While it is no longer playable, it still holds pride of place in the church, and the rather small electronic keyboard, which is now used regularly, is found skulking and a little embarrassed with itself off to one side.

We still had some more time before we needed to return to the ship, so our very kind driver took us up to the remains of an industrial plant where Labradorite used to be prepared. Labradorite is a feldspar mineral that shows beautiful blue scintillations, aptly called Labrador-escence. The rock is found in an area south of Nain and used to be shipped to Hopedale for preparation before sale. At one time this finished and polished rock was in demand in Europe, because of its beauty, but with the downturn of the economy about four years ago (2010) the plant went bankrupt and the pieces of rock were just left where they lay. Looking at the beauty of this rock, I hope at some point it will be recognized for the attractive stone it is, and the people of Hopedale will be able to reopen the plant and start to sell the rock once more. The large sheets of whole and broken pieces were just piled or scattered around the area, and we were able to pick up some small samples as souvenirs of Hopedale. According to our guide, the Assembly House here in Hopedale is a must-see because the floor of the main assembly room is paved with this very attractive rock.

The Hopedale Assembly House, reminiscent of an igloo and with an inuksuk at its crest

To complete our tour, our guide offered to drive the group out to the 'airport'. Bob and I opted for a walk back to the ship, with a quick browse through the local 'everything' store. As always, the store was a crazy amalgam of things to buy, and filled us with wonderment about the stock. Why just one single package of boy's underwear but a small army of socks? Do they really need two full shelves of towels of various sizes while not carrying, right now, a single ball of string? (We desperately needed string to hang up my freshly-washed underwear in the cabin.) How many shower curtains can one village need? I was tempted to buy one to take back with me, since there was an amazing range of them. Needless to say, we didn't buy anything, but we came away smiling at this crazy, mixed up store. No doubt, as the summer goes on, there will be a many more items on their shelves. Yes, at one level we find this pastime of ours amusing, but we know of course that the wondrously eclectic stock of these remote communities speaks volumes of life on the edge. They are a sort of touchstone to the way of life, so our fascination with window shopping is also a kind of research.

We walked slowly back to the ship after all our adventures at Hopedale. As we passed the dock I noticed that the granite rocks in the water had wonderful swirling patterns and colours in them, caused by distortion while undergoing metamorphosis during the pre-Cambrian era. The variety of rocks and the ever-changing land and seascape makes for some interesting effects, and just seeing the water wash over the rocks, bringing out their colour and pattern, was both beautiful and unusual.

Once back on board we stayed on deck watching as the ship headed out to sea once more. We were chatting with a retired fisherman and his wife from Newfoundland, and as it became quite chilly and foggy, the four of us retired to the cafeteria, which was open although supposed to be closed. We continued our interesting conversation and they told us about their trip to Ottawa a few years ago when he had required major cardiac surgery. The staff of the Ottawa Hospital were lauded for all their care and attention, which resulted in this fine gentlemen returning to Newfoundland in much better health. He told us about his earlier job as a fisherman, but now he runs a business hiring boats and skippers to go fishing for him, while he sells their catch. There was nostalgia in the way he spoke about the past, and we could feel his desire to be back on the ocean catching his own fish, but at the same time he was realistic about his ability to do that. The conversation soon segued into a discussion on the state of the world, the importance of basic food security in Canada, and of course politics. Fortunately, we were all like-minded so this discussion was very friendly and rewarding.

At one point during our conversation, one of the many small-sized kids on board came up to me and started being a bit silly. Both Bob and I had talked to her before, and when we were ready to move on she would run off. But this time was different; she just hung around, so I asked if she wanted company, and the answer was "Yes," so we cuddled and talked briefly, until her older sister found her and took her off to their cabin. A pleasant interlude with a cute kid.

We had one more stop before we made it to Nain and our turnaround point. As we were due to dock in Natuashish at midnight, we had no plans to go ashore on this visit. The ship would stop there on its return journey, so we knew we could see the place then. Our only concern was being disturbed by the regular announcements prior to docking. There were always three announcements over the loudspeakers, which allowed passengers time to get themselves organized to disembark. However, on this occasion we slept right through them!

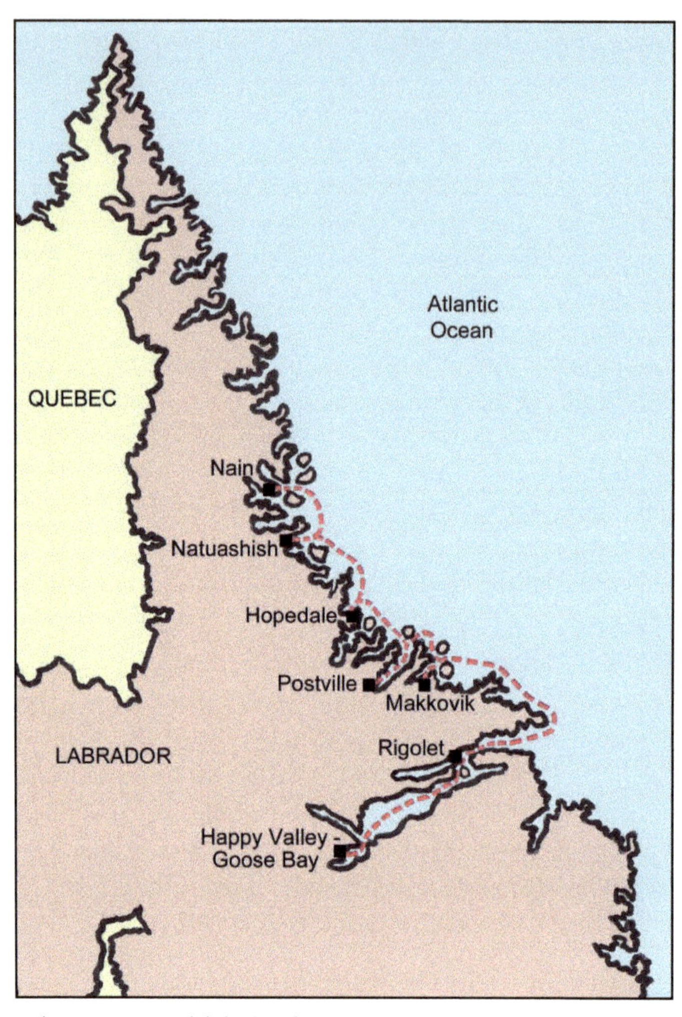

Nain to Natuashish (and return)	124nm
Natuashish to Hopedale (and return)	114nm
Hopedale to Postville	62nm
Postville to Makkovik	40nm
Makkovik to Rigolet	147nm
Rigolet to Goose Bay	86nm
TOTAL	573nm

Chapter Five
Hopedale to Nain and back to Happy Valley-Goose Bay

Finally, we arrived in Nain, the furthest point north on our travels. Our vessel docked at around 12:30pm and we were free to wander around the town for the next few hours. As we walked down the gangplank into Nain it felt a little odd, almost anticlimactic, knowing we would now be heading generally south for the rest of our travels. But it was time to explore as much as we could of Nain, and learn more about this very different part of Canada.

As at other ports, friends and relatives greeted the ship

And so our explorations of this, our most northern port of call, started. Our first encounter, straight off the ship, was with a peddler selling earrings and necklaces. He was apparently a well-known figure at the dock, and also the airstrip, and he made his living carving soapstone jewelry for the tourist trade. His work was very fine and I bought a pair of inuksuk earrings, very much a symbol of this area, and have worn them many times since then, bringing back so many memories of this area. I later learned that he also sold his jewelry to the craft store in Nain, which would expose his work to a somewhat larger market.

After purchasing the earrings we continued to the old Moravian church. We really would have liked to see the inside but it was locked and, it seems, had been for quite some time. We contented ourselves with photographing it from the outside. Apparently, the Moravian community had moved their mission up onto the hill over the town and no longer used this pretty looking church, so we hoped a way would be found to maintain and preserve it as an example of the early churches of the locale.

The little Moravian church with its Rhenish helm steeple, a most unusual feature for this part of the world

Nain was a much bigger place that the previous ports we had visited, so there was more to see. We had been told about a lovely craft store, so together with some of our friends from the ship, we went looking for it. After walking up some very steep roads—Nain is built on the side of a hill—we located the store. Unfortunately it was closed. We were rather disappointed, and started to walk back down the street until we heard someone calling us. We looked around and there was a young woman coming down the hill quickly towards us. She introduced herself as the Executive Director of the Community Centre building that included the craft store, and she was coming right now to open up for visitors from the ship.

This young woman had been newly appointed. Her husband was originally from Nain. They had met in St John's and had recently moved to back to Nain with their young child. She had found work in the Community Centre, and through her efforts in the Centre she had been able to stimulate its growth, making it a more active place, establishing the craft shop outlet, and other services for the community. While she was talking with us her employee added his comments, and agreed that the work this young woman was doing was positive for the community. We spent quite some time with them discussing their community, and they were able to enlighten us about the activities available in the winter, which was something we had been wondering about. Among other features, the Community Centre has an arena, and during the winter a very active hockey association arranges for teams to travel to a number of tournaments in a variety of locations up and down the coast. And we just thought the population would be totally isolated through the winter months!

While it was clear to us that living in these remote areas does bring many challenges, throughout our conversation it was clear that she loved living here. As an example of the challenges she embraced, she described a period when the water supply was compromised so she had bought a two-litre container of orange juice at a cost of $14.00. This was just for her young son who needed something safe to drink. She had seen members of the community going out to collect water, but did not know how safe it was. Later on she discovered that the water was from a clean spring coming down the hillside, so in future if she needs to she knows she can collect her water from there.

While on the ship we had met a young couple who were anxious to find their way to the Torngat Mountains National Park to do some wildlife photography. We were skeptical about their plans, as they didn't seem to have any solid information or any idea of how to go about getting there. So, during the course of our conversation with the staff of the craft store we happened to mention this young couple. They told us how difficult it is to get to the Torngat; Parks Canada is very active in controlling access to the park for safety reasons, and there are only two ways of getting to the mountains: either flying or taking a seven-hour ride by boat. Also, everyone entering the Park is obliged to employ a bear guard, and this is carefully monitored. Hikers are not permitted to just walk in, as this young couple seemed to hope, especially without a bear guard. So the staff felt it was very unlikely they would get permission to enter the Park in the remainder of the very short summer season. While is seemed a shame they would fail, it made sense to us. This is a very large and wild area, and it is very easy to get lost. Also, the risk of polar bear and wolf attack is great in these wild areas, hence the need for bear guards. We were told of a polar bear that stalked a kayak for three days as its owners paddled up the coast. When the bear was finally noticed the party tried to unsuccessfully to scare him off, but he was determined to follow, which sadly resulted in him being shot and killed. On examination, the bear was totally starved and it was this desperation that found him stalking the kayak in the hopes of a square meal! It is stories like this that remind us of the challenges of living here.

While we were with the Community Centre staff we mentioned how much we enjoyed going to the local stores because they encapsulate and epitomize their communities. It is easy to see what supplies are readily available and their cost. Maybe there are only very brown bananas, I said, or perhaps rather sad looking lettuce, and maybe only one head of lettuce anyway. Socks are always plentiful, and it seems that most of these stores carry bathroom linens in great supply. Do you need hardware, need to paint your house, what about canning those Labrador bakeapples? You may find your supplies there. They agreed about the often eclectic mix of supplies, and when they run out of something, they can only wait for the supply ship, however long it takes. As a result of this little give-and-take they directed us to the two stores in town to continue our 'research'.

The first store had a variety of foods, including some nice ham, which we bought. Yes, it was twice the price of the same thing in Ottawa, but it was a long way from the original production line and the transportation costs had to be taken into consideration. Bob needed a battery for his mouse, but this place had none, one of those funny little lacks. Perhaps there had been a run on batteries for some reason or other? Then it was off to the Northern Store, a place we have explored in several other places, including Moosonee and Inuvik. And, as with those other Northern Stores, this one had the usual wondrous mix of supplies. Food, paint, clothing, including underwear (which I happily bought), batteries for Bob's mouse, boots, shoes, etc. were all part of the mix. If you need anything, they try to supply it, but it is all dependent on the ships servicing the area.

By the time we had finished exploring the Northern Store and sharing a laugh with the cashier about the story behind my purchase of underwear, we went back to the ship. It was a very warm day, and we didn't need our jackets, so after leaving them back on the ship we walked over to watch the fishermen catching Arctic Char at the dock and preparing it for drying for the winter season. While we were observing this activity, we noticed a couple of brave young girls jumping in and out of the water near the dock.

Not the sort of temperature we like for bathing!

After admiring their courage in facing the very cold ocean water, we decided to explore more of Nain, so headed off in the direction of the airport. Like all 'airports' in this part of the world, it comprised one small strip and taxiway, only really suitable for very small planes. We watched as a Twin Otter was being prepared for takeoff, waiting until it was airborne before turning towards the dock once more.

The Twin Otter is the workhorse of all Canada's remote places

As we made our way back we stopped by two older men who were building a dory out of plywood. We asked them if the young people were interested in learning this art, and they shook their heads. It appears this is just one of the many skills that are being lost, a vivid reminder of the conversation we had had with the young women in North West River earlier in our travels.

The simple construction of the dory is evident here. Old Skidoo tracks make useful walkways; we saw them in use in several places

The MV *Northern Ranger* was almost ready to leave, so we hurried back on board and watched and waited while the last few things were loaded into the hold. The dockside was crowded, which surprised us until we realized there were many friends and relatives waiting to say goodbye to their loved ones. As the ship left, the whole dock was waving and shouting goodbye to all on board.

As the ship steamed away from Nain, we spotted a polar bear along the rocky shoreline. It only took a few seconds before we realized, with much amusement, it was merely a white rock in the shape of a bear. Was this just a fluke of nature, or had someone added it to the scenery to fool us tourists? Who knows? We left laughing at ourselves and our mistake!

Our brief visit to Nain was enjoyable and informative, and by actually being there we developed a greater understanding of the issues facing the people in this part of the world. Now, when I hear about troubling weather in Labrador, I am better able to imagine its effect on these very isolated communities. We were discussing our experiences with one of the crew members, and he agreed about some of the very real issues the communities had to cope with. For example, alcohol in a concern for these isolated villages, as it is in many other places. In an effort to combat this, RCMP officers examine everything coming in and out of the communities, looking mainly for alcohol, but also for illegal substances. So when the ships arrive at the dock, the officers check not only the freight, but also the baggage the residents bring in. When traveling we are used to having our bags searched by customs officials of the country we are entering, but we hardly realized that this was a reality here, and it made us think a lot more deeply about the local issues. Having worked in a field where addictions issues were a concern, I am aware of the violence and tragedy that can occur when they come into play, so it made a lot of sense to be proactive in trying to combat this scourge. When we were told that a gallon of liquor could be sold for around a $1,000 we were shocked and a little horrified. It may be lucrative, but the cost of importing booze will likely result in the loss of a job, especially if the guilty parties are employed on one of the supply ships.

There is work here in Labrador, but people have to travel to find it. The hydroelectric development at Muskrat Falls and the nickel mine in Voisey's Bay both provide good jobs and good pay, but the downside is the work schedule. Given the distances the employees need to travel, the schedule is intense; two weeks on and two weeks off. And while this makes sense in terms of work hours, in many cases it creates family tensions as a result of the ever-changing family dynamics. Yet another idea to try to get our heads around.

After leaving Nain the vessel returned south revisiting the communities in reverse order, which meant our first stop on this return leg was Natuashish. We docked at around 8:00pm and saw for the first time what it actually meant to the disembarking passenger as the RCMP officers came on board to search for contraband. For Bob and me, even though we understood the reasons, it felt very intrusive and positively un-Canadian. Even more of a surprise was that those leaving the ship simply took it for granted! This scrutiny is a necessary evil.

The approach to Natuashish harbour

Natuashish itself is over 3km from the dock, and since none of us tourists had transportation we wondered if we would be able to explore the village. Little did we know that it would not have been a good idea. When one of the RCMP officers at the dock offered to drive a few of us into town and show us around, we leapt at the opportunity. The officer took us in two groups, the number in each group being limited by the seating of his cruiser, and since we were in the second group we spent our time enjoying the peacefulness of the dock at sunset. When the officer returned with the first group about half an hour later it was our turn, and we were off on a very different type of exploration. I chose to forgo the experience of sitting in the back of the cruiser, having experienced that once before when discussing work-related information with an officer. The whole experience had been a little unnerving, so I sat in the front while Bob and the others enjoyed the confines of the back seat, with its wire mesh screen and no handles on the locked doors. Like me, they found the experience unique, since most law-abiding individuals don't usually end up the back of a police cruiser!

The first port of call was the town dump; a couple of the group had never seen black bears in the wild, and this open dump, like others of its ilk, attracted a variety of wildlife, in particular the bears and some feral dogs. This was not the most attractive area, and even though we were able to spot a big black bear rooting around the garbage, it was a sad spectacle. The dogs were everywhere, looking remarkably healthy given their somewhat unpleasant diet. Apparently, the local Animal Rescue comes by at various times, collects the dogs and tries to find homes for them. Whether this is successful or not, I don't know. The bears, large and small, are left to their own devices. At one point the authorities did try relocating them, but found they always returned to the dump. After this inauspicious start to our tour, it was on to Natuashish itself.

Bob and I found this a very disturbing experience. Over the years we have visited other First Nations communities, and although most of them had some social issues, generally speaking they seemed to function reasonably well. Sadly, Natuashish is not one of these. As he drove to the village, the officer gave us a brief history of this community. Originally, this had been an organized and functioning population of hunter gatherers living a nomadic life around Davis Inlet. Then, for whatever reason, the community was relocated to this area, newly-named Natuashish, and was forbidden to hunt or fish other than for subsistence, thus taking away their traditional way of life and replacing it with nothing. Now it is a smallish community of about 900 people, over half of whom are under the age of 18. The only work available is at the store, in the hospital and, naturally, at the Band Council. Because the people of this community are unable to follow their traditional ways of hunting or fishing, there are very few activities for this tiny population to become involved with. To make things worse, it was decided that all royalties earned on the natural resources extracted from their land would be paid to the residents directly in cash. This all works to create a very dysfunctional society. The houses are all owned by the Band, and the families occupy them free of charge. As with any community, some of the houses look to be in a reasonable state of repair, while others appear very rundown. Most of the public buildings has been vandalized. We had no idea, of course, what it was like inside the homes. The police officer described serious issues of alcohol abuse, as well as other substances, hence the effort to keep the place as dry as possible. Just to press home this point, while he was driving us back to the dock he received a call to pick up a woman who was dead drunk and lying on a driveway.

Needless to say, I really did not enjoy this visit; while it was an eye-opening experience, it also made me feel very sad, and continues to make me wonder what can be done to allow our Native communities to redevelop their own very valuable human resources.

It was quite late when we returned to the dock. We noticed the gangplank was closely guarded by the ship's crew to prevent uninvited guests coming aboard—another reflection of this particular stop on the voyage—and we were told that it would be raised at 10:00pm, a couple of hours prior to departure. While this seemed very harsh to us, it reflected the reality and tragedy of this very troubled community.

It was still light and quite warm that evening, so we watched a large crowd of children who were just hanging out on the dock. One of the young girls was driving a four-wheeler around with a passenger holding on. It was a crazy ride and we watched with our hearts in our mouths as she did 'donuts' at great speed, weaving around the groups of children, driving onto the dock and turning sharply just before she would plunge into the water. While she was obviously a skilled driver, it was nerve wracking to watch because we anticipated that one small error could have disastrous consequences. It was a relief when she finally left, but one had to wonder where the adults in the community were who could help the young people to grow up and act in a responsible way. There are always good people in any community, and this one is no exception, but according to the police they are in the minority. All of us were glad to leave Natuashish because it was distressing to see, and for both of us there was a feeling of frustration due to the many years of governmental policies that have created such situations. Having just read Thomas King's *The Inconvenient Indian* and the long history of the decisions the governments of both Canada and the USA have made regarding the indigenous population, the situation we saw in Natuashish starts to make much more tragic sense.

A nice sunset picture taken from the dock just before we left Natuashish; a contrast of beauty with squalor

Thankfully, our home on the seas left Natuashish while we were peacefully sleeping and arrived back in Hopedale early next morning. This felt like a much better place to be. So, remembering what our erstwhile tourist guide had told us, we went ashore and headed for the

Assembly Building. This very attractive structure, very reminiscent of an igloo, overlooks the bay, and we had noticed it as we came into the dock on our first visit (see p. 53). On the top of the building, in what might be thought of as the bell tower, there is a large inuksuk overlooking the village and the harbour. We entered the foyer, which was beautifully lit by windows on three sides that allowed the natural light in. After a brief look around we found the boardroom, a beautifully appointed space with a floor of Labradorite and granite, quite beautiful. The walls were hung with a variety of pictures showing various aspects of the life of the village, and we spent some time just enjoying them.

The boardroom of the Assembly Hall. This picture cannot do justice to the appearance of the labradorite floor

Then we crossed over to the Assembly Hall, and here we appreciated our tour guide's advice about the floor. It was stunning. The entire floor was polished Labradorite, and the small blue flecks in the stone scintillated in the light. As we just stood there admiring the floor and the rest of the room, we suddenly realized that the sound we could hear from outside was the ship's horn calling us back. We left the Assembly

Building quickly, thankful to have seen that gorgeous floor. We found it interesting to note the differences in the way that the band councils of Natuashish and Hopedale had spent the royalties derived from natural resource extraction on their land.

Making our way out to sea on the way back to Postville it felt as if we were in iceberg alley. There were any number of bergs in the distance, and it seemed as if every time we scanned the horizon, we would catch sight of more. They were much too far away to photograph, but wonderful to see in binoculars, and they certainly met our hopes and expectations. And then, as the icing on the cake, some whales were seen swimming quite near the vessel. They didn't stick around, but showed themselves briefly and then swam on. They were obviously too busy to demonstrate all their wonderful moves for us, but just seeing them as we traveled was a rewarding experience and completely fulfilled our hope of seeing more than just one whale. By this time the weather had become quite beautiful, the sea as calm as glass and the sun shining; as perfect a day at sea as anyone could want.

The closest of the many icebergs we saw

As we watched out for other sea life (we were just greedy to see as much as we could), a crew member invited a few of the passengers up to the bridge. We met the Third Mate and other crew members on the bridge, who took turns in explaining the functions of all the various navigation tools. Apparently, all the equipment is duplicated so if one item fails there is a backup, a reassuring thought for all us passengers. Bob was given the opportunity to steer the ship for a couple of minutes, which he really enjoyed, and he didn't ground it on any rocks! I was also given the opportunity to do the same, but let Bob have the experience, since so many years ago I had actually steered a cargo ship up the St Lawrence, heading towards Montreal (see p. 8). We spent some time up there on the bridge talking to the crew, but as the ship neared Postville, it was time to leave and let them bring us safely into dock.

As had now become our habit, once we had docked and the gangplank was down, we went for a walk. We were pleased to meet our companion from a few days back, the Postville teacher, and so chatted with her for a while, before wandering around the village just to stretch our legs before a return to the ship. It was such a wonderfully warm day that, on our return to the ship, we climbed the stairs to the upper deck and relaxed in the sun on deckchairs. As the ship left the dock we noticed perfect circles of disturbed water, and discovered we were seeing harbour seals popping their little heads up to breathe. They were busy doing what seals do, so that was all we could see of them, and even this was only because the sea was incredibly calm, making the small ripples their little heads made actually visible. Several of the passengers and crew commented on the calmness of the seas, and it sounded to us that this was a little unusual. It just felt and looked like sailing on a calm lake in the middle of Ontario!

Now we were almost home, heading towards Makkovik and then Rigolet, the last two stops before arriving back in Goose Bay. However, as we sat in the cafeteria enjoying our supper we heard news of some icebergs floating by, fairly close to the ship. So after we had eaten we went back on deck to see if they were close enough to have their picture taken. The bergs were still a long way off, but closer than the others we had seen, so fortunately were able to memorialize these bergs in pixels with some halfway decent pictures.

The experience of seeing these huge natural wonders is quite something. It is hard to describe the emotions it elicits. They are so big, and they look so purposeful as they drift on by, that it seems as if they know exactly where they are going. Seeing them from the ship was a joy, close enough to enjoy, yet far enough away to feel safe. As I have mentioned previously, when planning this voyage of discovery back in Ottawa we had hoped to see icebergs, but as it would be nearly August we really didn't hold out much hope, so this was certainly a bonus and we really appreciated the experience.

Once on shore in Makkovik we immediately became the source of a good meal for the local bugs, so we cut our walk short and headed back to the ship. As we were walking back along the road to the harbour we encountered a local fisherman smoking salmon in his smokehouse on the beach. We chatted with him briefly, and he described the various ways of smoking salmon and other fish, and then spoke very movingly about the loss of his son nearly two years ago. It was clear this still affected both him and his family, and we felt touched that he would share so personal an experience with us.

A rudimentary but very effective smokehouse parked up the beach from the fishing boats

As we came closer to the pier we noticed it was full of activity, with several fishing boats seemingly ready to go out to sea. We were curious about their catch and learned that crab was in season, and they were off to fill the holds of their boats. This reminded us of the frozen crab from this area we had seen being loaded into the hold a couple of days ago. These fishermen also go out after shrimp and turbot, depending on the season, which no doubt helps the economy of this little place.

One of the many seascapes that we feasted our eyes on

Our final stop of the trip was Rigolet, quite early in the morning, so after a brief walk I went back to the cabin to pack our things ready for our return to Happy Valley-Goose Bay. We considered briefly whether to extend our voyage for a couple more days by traveling down the coast to Cartwright and back, but we finally decided against it. We were beginning to feel the pressure of moving on to the next stage of our journey, and that involved starting the trek to Red Bay on the southern coast of Labrador.

While I was packing, Bob had the wonderful experience of being invited by the Chief Engineer to examine the working parts of the ship—the below-decks realm of the engine and mechanical rooms—so when we left Rigolet he was nowhere to be found. He appeared shortly afterwards out of the bowels of the ship with all kinds of stories about the engines and associated machinery. Every single aspect of the ship's functioning is controlled and monitored. Besides the main engines—

two great eight-cylinder diesels—there are machines for steering, air conditioning, lighting, pumping and heating water, sewage disposal and all the other myriad functions. The Chief was happy to describe the functioning of all the components in detail and was pleased with Bob's knowledge, albeit basic, of most of the bits and pieces. He got to walk alongside the engines and generators, and got close-up views of the working machinery. The noise was terrific. Bob was privileged to be present at start-up, when the ship began to leave the dock and the Captain on the bridge called for power. The Chief ranged over his monitors in the engine control room and stated that every aspect of the ship's functioning could be observed. "See the demand on the vacuum system for the toilets?" he remarked pointing at one of the gauges. "No surprise; it's just after breakfast so that's where most of them are." He also talked about the competition between the bridge and the engine room, and how in a small vessel like this it was all light-hearted and convivial, but in larger ships there could be real animosity and misunderstanding. What the Captain asks for and what the Chief can provide are sometimes two very different things, and managing this can be quite tricky. The tour concluded with a long climb up companion-ways to the upper deck of the ship where the emergency electric generator stood on stand-by, one of the many duplicate items of machinery that provide for a fail-safe operation at sea.

Now, on the final leg of this voyage, I settled in the salon with my knitting. An Inuit lady from Rigolet sat down beside me and asked if I had any playing cards she could borrow. Since I didn't have any, she stayed and we started to talk. She told me she was from Rigolet and was going to Goose Bay for a few days. We talked about her family and she proudly spoke about her son who had a permanent job through the summer, 40 hours a week with two days off, working on the dock in Rigolet. This was really important as it meant he would be eligible for Employment Insurance in the winter when the dock was closed down. Meanwhile, her daughter was working in St John as a parole officer. The daughter, she told me, had attended Memorial University and had a degree in psychology. I asked if her daughter would ever come back, and she thought not, but she does see her about once a year. She seemed very proud of how well her daughter was doing and told me that the daughter and her partner were buying a house there, so she felt they were well settled.

I was curious about living in the remote areas of Labrador in the winter and what kind of things they did for entertainment. She described the community hall, the arena, skidooing and so on, and said they also play a lot of cards and socialize quite a bit. It sounded to me as if the people in the community were very active and involved with each other. She told me that in the winter there are many tracks throughout the area, so getting around by skidoo is much easier than the same journeys in summer. Also, in the spring there is a big family gathering, with much feasting and the meeting of far flung members of the family.

The family food fish allowance is strictly regulated. Apparently, the number of fish caught remains the same per household irrespective of the number of people. Each household is allowed to catch only seven salmon, and a specific number of char. Basically, this allowance is fine for a small family, but for the larger families with lots of children it really isn't enough. They are not allowed to hunt caribou and, besides, she mentioned that the herd had not come through for a while. People are still allowed to hunt small animals, such as rabbit and the like. I described briefly a native woman from Inuvik we had met, who had hunted whale, as had her daughters. From the Inuit lady's reaction, I gathered this is type of hunting doesn't take place on this coast. We also spoke of preserving the fish by drying them and she indicated that they dry fast after being skinned and filleted. Also, her people will smoke, salt and pickle fish in order to keep them longer. After some time she got up in search of a deck of cards, and left me thinking of all the things she had talked about, including the issues with the stores and food shortages at various times. It was a wonderful discussion and I felt honoured to have spent so much time with her.

Now we were back in Melville Inlet, really close to Goose Bay, and it was all about waiting as the ship steamed slowly inland. So, after lunch the cabin was packed and we were ready to leave the ship. Once the announcement came over the loudspeakers, "Thirty minutes to arrival in Goose Bay," we went down to the disembarkation area and spent time chatting with our new-found friends, Michael and Linda, before we docked. Once on land it was into the RV and off to do all those necessary chores so we could leave the next morning and head south for the next part of the adventure.

Back in Goose Bay, our last view of the sea before driving inland

Our first stop was the bank where I had to complete all those routine monthly transactions. We sat down with a very helpful cashier who talked me through all the intricacies of using the bank's internet. While this was going on, Bob opened a conversation with her. Her husband was in the military and had been posted to Goose Bay for two years. They had only been here for a few months and seemed to be enjoying their experiences in Labrador. She had quickly found the job in the bank, which no doubt helped in her transition to the area. She had not been here long enough to go through a full winter period, and it would have been interesting to find out how she experienced that. We had had some difficulty with Wi-Fi in this area, and she agreed that it was a slow system, and even in the bank it was molasses-like! And for those living in the area, it was not easy to get hooked up with the system for their home; it took several months, quite unlike the service we take for granted in the south! We really appreciated her help with our banking, something we do almost without thinking at home, while the good conversation was an extra bonus we did not anticipate.

We had learned from our friends Mike and Linda that the government of Newfoundland and Labrador offers the free service of a satellite phone for travelers, which is an indication of the general understanding of the condition of the roads. We spent some time trying to get hold of one for our drive south to Red Bay, but it seems that demand outstrips supply and they are often not returned immediately, so we were unable to avail ourselves of this service. Our plan remained the same: we would drive towards Red Bay and hope nothing too serious occurred during our drive.

As we headed back to our campsite we kept thinking about our incredible experiences on the MV *Northern Ranger*, and the difference in the way we now thought of this area of our wonderful country.

Happy Valley-Goose Bay to Port Hope Simpson	421km
Port Hope Simpson to Mary's Harbour	57km
Mary's Harbour to Red Bay	88km
TOTAL	566km

Chapter Six
Happy Valley-Goose Bay to Red Bay

After our wonderful trip to Nain and all our experiences, we were ready to continue exploring this huge and empty part of Labrador. Our friends Mike and Linda were also planning to travel to Red Bay, and we had earlier planned to travel in convoy just to have the extra security of two vehicles, especially since neither of us could acquire a satellite phone. Unfortunately, our friends were both suffering with a cold bug, so they decided to take a recovery day and leave the following morning. We were anxious to get going, so we said goodbye to them at the campsite and started the trip south to Red Bay.

As we made our way to Highway 510 we wondered what this road would really be like. Given our earlier experiences with the roads of Labrador, we were a little nervous about the drive. We drove west out of Happy Valley-Goose Bay, turned onto the highway, and were pleasantly surprised by the quality of this gravel surface. We began to relax as we headed south towards Red Bay. The road surface was very good for unpaved gravel, and we were able to maintain relatively normal highway speeds, encountering only brief areas of roughness. So, for about 200km we drove happily along enjoying the scenery and wondering what all the fuss was about.

A long vista from the cab of the RV

We skirted the Mealy Mountains, visible in the distance to the east and north, and passed through a variety of types of vegetation, from forested areas to scrubland with a great many rocks. The road crossed many rivers, lakes and ponds which all appeared to be flowing north towards Lake Melville. We took a break at around noon, parked on the side of the road, and enjoyed our lunch while admiring the very rugged and empty scenery.

The sort of scene we encountered all day

Bob took over the driving in the afternoon and was enjoying his time at the wheel until we came close to the turnoff to Cartwright. We don't know why, but from here on the road deteriorated dramatically and the driving became unspeakable. We later learned that the section of the highway between Red Bay and Cartwright is the most frequently traveled, and thus the amount of traffic is detrimental to the road surface. Whatever the reason, the conditions were appalling and our speed and comfort deteriorated in tandem, and when we thought it couldn't get any worse, it did! Bob was finding his way around really nasty surfaces; washboard was the main culprit, but then we came across large rocks sticking up, potholes between the rocks, loose gravel and anything else you can imagine. The dust was also a never-ending presence and the nonstop vibration caused everything to shake! And all this when our top speed varied between 25 and 40kph, although for the most part it was closer to the lower figure. The poor van gave new meaning to the expression 'shake, rattle and roll'. It did all of that and more besides. As usual, the chesterfield cushions took their walk around the van and met their old friend the kitchen rug. The drawers and cupboards all had extra bungees to try and keep them shut (we were learning!) but they still tried to join the dance of the sugarplum cushions, but thankfully were not as successful this time! We did stop a couple of times to switch the driving responsibilities, and on one of these brief pauses we noticed a leak in the drainage system! The road had taken its toll! The good thing about this 'incident' was that the pipe was the grey water and not the black, so we were merely watering the road (which could only improve it) and not contaminating it! Initially, we thought it was merely a small leak due to the vibration, but on closer examination with an angled mirror, Bob found a good sized hole in the drainpipe, no doubt due to the rocks on the road bouncing off it on a regular basis. We were very surprised that black ABS, a very tough material, could be damaged in such a way. It just demonstrated the issues we had met on this lovely highway. Later on, Bob was able to fix the hole on a temporary basis with duct tape (the handyman's secret weapon) and a couple of zip-ties! But a full repair had to wait for a few days until we could find a store with the necessary hose clamps and waterproof tape for doing a better job.

The rocks beside the road and the rocks in it. Often indistinguishable

After what seemed like eons, we finally made it into Port Hope Simpson, took our shattered nerves over to a lovely little café overlooking the shoreline, and enjoyed a resuscitative cup of tea. While we were chatting to the staff we were given directions to the town's designated camping area, which offered free sites with water hook-ups.

This sounded like a good option since we were tired and really didn't feel like driving any further. We found the place and pulled in. It looked really pleasant, the only downside being the lack of electrical hook-ups. Normally this wouldn't have worried us, and given the coolness of the weather we had experienced previously, we hardly thought ventilation would be needed. However, this day was uncharacteristically very hot and humid, and without either an external power supply or opening the windows, we thought it might get quite hot through the night. While we were debating this I stepped outside and became closely acquainted with the local blackfly population. The place was thick with them. That did it! A very brief discussion and perusal of all our tourist information found us heading to the local hotel with its air conditioning, and the happy abandonment of our blackfly friends. The hotel overlooked a coastal inlet, and after a nice relaxing supper we were able to connect with WiFi, and thus keep in touch with the outside world.

One of the joys of traveling in an RV is the people you meet and re-meet along the way. This night was no exception. As we went in for supper we met a Swiss family we had originally met on the ship from Nain. We had chatted to them briefly during that week, so it was nice to see them again and learn about their ongoing plans. Then, just as we were finishing supper, our friends Mike and Linda showed up. We were surprised to see them, knowing how miserable they had been in the morning, but now they were a walking advert for the power of both Tylenol and Advil to make a body feel better. We chatted with them briefly and they told us that once they had felt a little better, all they wanted to do was get moving.

After a good night's sleep and a wonderful breakfast in the hotel we were ready to face the road again. One of the destinations in our mound of tourist information was Battle Harbour, so we planned to drive to Mary's Harbour to find out more about it. If we liked what we heard, we would try to go over there for the day on the ferry service that was mentioned in the brochure. Mary's Harbour is about 50km from Port Hope Simpson, so we allowed an ample two hours to get there in order to catch the Battle Harbour ferry, which left at 11:00am. Our GPS suggested it would take less than an hour but, as we had discovered, while Madame GPS knew about the road, she had never actually seen it, let alone driven it. And so we started on what would become a very 'interesting' part of Highway 510.

We were advised by other travelers that the surface was 'not that great', which concerned us only a little. In view of the driving we had already experienced, how could it be any worse? It was, and the least said about it the better! We had allowed two hours to drive these 50km, and at one point we really didn't think we would make it in time for the ferry! We left Port Hope Simpson before 9:00am, and with our average speed of probably around 20kph, the numbers weren't working in our favour. One of Bob's more amusing comments related to his time in sub-Saharan Africa, where the drivers would leave the road and drive along the side, since it was easier and safer. He wished we could repeat that experience here in Labrador. We were actually happy to see muddy sections because we could increase our speed to above 20kph, making it somewhat easier and more comfortable. We needed more mud and less of the rocks, potholes and washboard!

A welcome rest beside the road at midday

The concentration needed to drive this portion was intense. During my stints I weaved all over the road trying to find slightly smoother bits to drive on. If Bob spoke to me I was not aware of it, as every part of my brain was focused on the road! At one point we were passed by two motorbikes, and as they wove their way around the worst areas we wondered what they thought of the conditions. As the clock continued ticking down, we were beginning to wonder if we would even make it to Mary's Harbour, never mind being in time for the ferry, or even deciding whether to go over to Battle Harbour anyway.

Finally, just as we were resigned to missing the ferry and a possible visit to Battle Harbour, the surface improved as did my speed, and we eventually made it to the small ferry terminal at 10:40am, a mere 20 minutes before the ferry was due to leave. By this time I was totally exhausted and just ready to stop and do nothing. After parking, or should I say, dumping the van we rushed down to the ferry office and checked with the staff about our choices. There were two ways of getting to Battle Harbour: the overnight trip at a total cost $400.00 all inclusive, or a privately owned boat for a day trip at $150.00 in cash. For this second choice we would need to get back in the RV, drive off to find the ATM somewhere in town, and then return to the ferry terminal. It seemed that the overnight stay was the best choice. The deal was sealed with the glad news that there was no blackfly on Battle Harbour Island, so within two minutes Bob was paying for the overnight trip, and I was back up to the RV to pack a bag for both of us. This was really diving into the unknown, and although having no real idea of what to expect we were ready for anything. The joy of not driving the RV any more that day was an incredible and very welcome bonus. (For information on Battle Harbour see Resources, p. 274.)

We were on the ferry by 11:00am with a small suitcase and a camera, and that was about it. It was a small boat with a cabin amidships, and a registered capacity of about 20 people, although on this day, there were only eight of us on board, including crew. It took us about 30 minutes to head out of the Mary's Harbour inlet, pass Great Caribou Island and the approach to Battle Harbour from the north. Until this point we didn't quite realize that Battle Harbour was on a small island off the coast and that the only way to get there was by boat. We had just thought it was inaccessible by road, so learning its true location was a revelation.

There were four other visitors on the boat; a couple who were touring and meeting friends and relatives of the wife, Cindy, whose family came from this area; and two bikers from Quebec, who had had passed us on the road. The bikers were an interesting pair. They were long-time friends and enjoyed taking trips on their bikes, and were now exploring Newfoundland and Labrador for the first time. We asked them about their impressions of the road. They had loved it! Their bikes had been fitted with extra shock absorbers to reduce the risk of damage and to enhance the ride, and being much more agile than a four-wheeled vehicle, they were able to manage the road more easily than us. This allowed them to avoid the really badly potholed and rough areas and, in short, they thoroughly enjoyed the experience!

Looking back at Mary's Harbour from the ferry

It was another beautiful day, sunny and warm with a calm and peaceful sea. On our way over to Battle Harbour some whales and harbour porpoises were swimming and playing a little way away, and there was a little iceberg floating relatively close to the boat, much closer than the ones we had seen while on the *Northern Ranger* several days earlier.

A baby iceberg, soon to melt away

As we rounded Great Caribou Island we approached Battle Harbour, and began to understand all the hype about this lovely little place. It is incredibly picturesque, with many small, colourful houses surrounded by grass, and nestled into a rocky island. Every so often, rocks could be seen breaking through the grass, as if to remind the inhabitants what their homes were built on! As we made our way into the tiny harbour we came alongside a large yacht, named *Latitude*, already docked. We learned later than this beautiful vessel had been chartered by two friends and outfitted as a dive boat. The group on board were planning to dive in as many of the major diving locations as they could, as well as sailing through the Northwest Passage and then down the west coast towards South America. *Latitude* had been commissioned originally by a Russian millionaire, and now was registered in the Cayman Islands and available for chartering (but just a little too pricey for our budget).

Approaching Battle Harbour from the sea

Battle Harbour has been an active player in the history of Labrador. While the records are not clear, it would appear to have been a working community since the 1770s. Because of its location with its easy access from the sea, it eventually came to be the unofficial capital of Labrador. Dr Wilfred Grenfell founded a nursing station on the Island in 1892, and the first Marconi stations were set up there in the early 20th century. The most famous moment of this wireless transmission station occurred in 1909 when Robert E. Peary, the Arctic explorer, telegraphed a report of his claim of reaching the North Pole.

Fishing played an important part in the history of this small island. In its early life there was an active fishing industry, which continued for many years but finally died with the Cod Moratorium in 1990. Since then, the Battle Harbour Historic Trust has worked to preserve and restore the historic buildings, rather than seeing them replaced, so the feel of an earlier time is maintained. The original houses, sheds, stores and workshops are now used in season for tourists to enjoy this beautiful place. Wiring, plumbing and heating has all been upgraded for safety reasons and comfort. And while cooking is not allowed in any of the buildings, most of them have a small kitchen area where guests can make tea or coffee and eat small snacks. It is not all about tourism, although that is an important part of Battle Harbour's economy; some original inhabitants still live on the island in homes which may have been in their families for several generations. These individuals are very active in everything that goes on, and in some instances are called upon to talk about the island from their personal experiences, which brings alive their stories and the history of the place.

We were taken directly from the ferry to the General Store, where guests checked in and learned where they would be sleeping that night. We were assigned the Rush Bendle room in the Merchants Building, named after one of the residents on the island. The room was quite beautiful and a very lovely surprise, being very different from anywhere else we have stayed. Our companions from the ferry were guests in other buildings; the bikers had the joy of the Bunkhouse, which was originally built for workers on the Island. They liked the idea of it, and enjoyed the experience.

The Rush Bendel room is typical of the accommodations at Battle Harbour; well appointed, very comfortable, and with a pleasant historical ambience

Meals were served in the loft above the General Store in a welcoming and warm space. Our arrival was timed for lunch, so once we had settled in, we found ourselves heading towards the loft where we were greeted with most welcome cups of tea and coffee. As I sat there with my tea, I could feel the tensions of the previous two days floating away in the breeze. It was a wonderful feeling, and I looked forward to 24 hours of luxury in paradise.

Shortly after we sat down, our meal was served by two very friendly ladies who did all the cooking and serving. Bob and the other guests were given a very rich and tasty seafood chowder with light and flaky biscuits, while they accommodated my shellfish allergy with a Jigg's Dinner. I had no idea what this entailed, so I was interested in discovering its components; salt beef, turnips, carrots, potatoes, cabbage and pease pudding. It was quite delicious and I really enjoyed it. Bob almost wished he could have tried it, but since the chowder was so good, he really didn't mind.

After lunch we met our guide, a local man who gave the group a really thorough tour of most of the public buildings on the island, and shared much of the island's history with us. He still lived on the island all year round, so he knew many snippets of information about it. Some of the people from the *Latitude* also joined the tour, which made it all the more interesting as we chatted to them about their interests. The tour took about an hour and then we were free to wander about this little island.

The main storehouse from the fish processing facility

As we climbed toward the highest point, we met one of the lovely ladies working here. She was carrying a number of containers filled with berries, and with the name Bob written on all of them. We laughed when we saw that and suggested that these containers must belong to Bob. She and her husband had been out picking bakeapples, and had filled these containers, so she offered us a taste. They were wonderful. It is hard to describe their flavour; sweet yet sharp, but smooth and creamy also describes them. She asked us if we would like some, and after our very rapid "Yes, please," she told us she would drop some over to our room. We thanked her and looked forward to receiving a small container.

The view from halfway up the hill. Our baby iceberg is just about visible

We continued our walk up the hill and met our motorcycle friends. As we followed the narrow paths threading between the rocks, we noticed all kinds of bakeapples growing on low bushes. These ones were not yet ripe, which is why they were still there. Here in Labrador, once they are ripe these precious wild fruits are picked right away. Now I realized how significant the information given to me in the Laundromat in Happy Valley-Goose Bay had been. Backapples are a really valuable commodity in this part of the world, and people treasure them. So to learn how to find them and pick them was a very caring kind of sharing.

These bakeapples are not quite ripe, which is why they are still on the bush

We made our way to the site of the first Marconi station in Labrador. The old facility has long since gone, and in its place there is a huge antenna. Standing there, with the wind coming off the ocean, and nothing much in sight except more sea, gave us a better understanding of why this spot was chosen; with the ocean on one side and the land on the other, it is the perfect place to site a communications station. Actually seeing and understanding the beginnings of telecommunication, especially in this area, made a huge impression on me, and finally learning this was the original station and main hub for radio transmission, was quite the eye opener.

As we walked further we found the remains of an old plane crash. We had been told about this accident, which occurred in 1986 and very much affected the people living on the island at that time. Bits of the plane are still visible, gently disintegrating naturally in the weather. The crash site was not discovered for several days, which seemed a little odd. But apparently nobody in this small community realized a plane was missing. Perhaps if they had heard about it earlier the outcome might have been different. Who knows? The memorial plaque on the rocky hill just added to the poignancy of the moment as we looked from the wreckage to the spectacular views from the top of the island. It was hard to reconcile the two. Walking down the hill still thinking about this tragedy, Mother Nature provided something to enjoy. As we looked out to sea we caught sight of a couple of porpoises and a whale swimming and playing in the water. What a contrast to the tragedy which had unfolded on that hill so many years ago.

As we headed back to our room our kindly lady handed us a one-litre yogurt container full of bakeapples. This wonderful gift was quickly placed in our small cooler, and would be a welcome and very different addition to our breakfast menu when on the road again. We were tired after all our travels of the day, so as we sat down with a cup of tea we reflected on our morning drive and marveled at how long ago that appeared to be! Now it was time for supper. Of course, in our rush to make the ferry we had only packed the bare necessities (including underwear); just a simple change of clothes for the next day. As the afternoon moved into the evening the temperature started to drop and the rain came in, and I thought how nice it would be to have a pair of jeans, instead of just shorts! Never mind, we were at Battle Harbour and it was all good.

As we entered the loft for supper we were surprised to find it quite crowded. Some of the crew from the *Latitude* had joined us, along with two gentlemen from Singapore and New York, lifelong friends who had leased the yacht along with one of the wives. Then there were other couples spending time on the island, making it a much bigger and noisier crowd than we had experienced at lunch. Finally, we met were the crew of a yacht sailing from Norway to Duluth, Minnesota by way of Iceland, Greenland and Newfoundland. Bob enjoyed spending time talking to one of the crew who had been an oarsman on the 1990s crossing of the Atlantic in a reproduction Viking longship. He had some very interesting tales to tell of the rigors of the crossing, although he did praise the quite un-Viking-like radio communications!

After a lovely supper of crab cakes (salad for me), turbot on risotto, and cheesecake with bakeapple topping—almost all of which was either locally produced or freshly caught—it was time for people to be 'Screeched In'.

This well-founded Newfoundland ceremony had a distinctly Labrador theme. First the boots have to be put on, then the mitts and for some the woolly hat. Then it's time to kiss the cod, or in this case a fillet of cod, eat a spoonful of bakeapples, and finally down a shot of Screech. (Screech is the raw rum that for centuries Newfoundland fishers traded for cod with Caribbean sugar planters.) Once this ritual has been performed, each person has to take the 'oath', an amusing little piece of poetry. Sort of. The penalty for reading this doggerel too slowly is to drink another shot of Screech and then read it again. How drinking more Screech would help, I still don't know; still, only a couple of young men had that difficult chore to complete. When it was my turn I changed the doggerel a little to suit me (it was quite gendered!) and the crowd enjoyed that. Fortunately, I only had to read it the once, and there was no penalty for changing the text! It was a lot of fun, and most of the guests were 'Screeched In' that evening, including Bob. He cheated a little, since he had taken the ceremony when working in Newfoundland several years ago. He justified this repeat performance by saying that mainland Labrador was different from the Rock, and therefore it needed doing again! Now we were both honorary Newfoundlanders.

The loft with its inviting lights beckoning us to dinner

Having enjoyed the silliness of the 'Screeching In' ceremony, we had the pleasure of two local musicians who arrived with a guitar and accordion and played lots of music of the region, encouraging the guests to join in and sing. Surprisingly, given the time of year (they usually show up at Christmas), the mummers came for a brief time, which created a lot of laughs. I think they had their dates confused, or was it the Screech? It was all a lot of fun to see them running around the room in their strange costumes and dancing to the music.

After a long set, the musicians took a break and Johnny, the gentlemen from New York, charterer of the *Latitude*, picked up the guitar with permission from its owner, and started playing and singing. He was really accomplished and the crowd loved it. I was sitting near him, so when he started singing one of my favourite Tom Paxton songs, "The Last Thing on my Mind", I joined in very quietly, since I really can't sing. He noticed, glanced over to me, and soon the song became a duet. It was magical. As we were both singing, me almost silently, I was totally living in this wonderful moment, and didn't realize the whole room had paused and was watching, seeing and enjoying the moment. In retrospect, I still can't believe it actually happened, and when I think of it, it seems like a dream.

Our musicians for the evening, with guest Johnny from New York

The seagoing crew were a little concerned by the reports of Bertha, the second hurricane of the season brewing. Since it was getting late and the *Latitude* would leave early the next morning in an effort to outrun this storm, the crew headed back to their ship to prepare for their early start. Gradually the party broke up and as we wandered back to our lovely Rush Bendle room, we thought over our amazing day. It had started with horrendous roads and finished with a most magical moment. What a day!

The next morning was cool, grey and windy, although not actually raining, and such a contrast to the perfect weather of the day before. We packed up our meagre belongs, carefully ensuring our precious bakeapples would make the trip back to the van safely, and then enjoyed breakfast in the Loft. We met our fellow travelers from the ferry, as well as a couple who we had noticed the previous evening, and we all discussed our plans for the next couple of days. As we had come to expect in this lovely place, breakfast was quite delicious; eggs Benedict on smoked salmon biscuits, a good start to our morning. We really didn't want to leave and were tempted to stay just one more night, but that was not to be. So we enjoyed our last couple of hours in this peaceful place as we prepared to travel on. After picking up some small souvenirs in the General Store we were ready to leave. The small yacht from Norway had already left and the *Latitude* was about to set sail, while our ferry waited to take us back to Mary's Harbour and reality.

Once again, there were only a few of us aboard, and as we left the lee of the land we found the beautiful and calm seas of the previous day had given way to agitated waters picked up by the wind, to which the boat responded by rocking and rolling and pitching herself through the waves. By many standards it was not a rough sea, but in contrast to the previous day it was not at all comfortable. It was also colder, so ill-clad legs longed for a pair of jeans. My shorts just weren't sufficient! We were still able to spot many more icebergs far off to the east, slowly moving in stately fashion, but probably being pushed a little faster by the wind. It was the end of a wonderful interlude and one I would recommend to anyone coming to this area.

Once we docked at Mary's Harbour we said goodbye to all our traveling companions, climbed back into the RV and started on the last piece of the highway, heading towards Red Bay and hoping the road would have magically improved. This was not to be. Bob was driving, which gave me a much appreciated break, and he had to cope with the usual conditions. However, we did encounter more than a ray of hope for the future of Highway 510: construction! Long sections of the road were being blasted and bulldozed preparatory to widening and re-surfacing. We were stopped for single-lane traffic a number of times as travelers came from the other direction, or large pieces of yellow roadwork machinery were manoeuvered across our path. The respite from slow, rattling driving was actually quite welcome, even though the peace of the big outdoors was filled with the rumble and roar of construction work. Once past this ongoing and welcome improvement for visitors to Labrador, we crept our way down to Red Bay, at times only doing about 25kph! It was still a brutal drive, with both us and the van shaken and rattled and bounced, and generally turned inside out! It really was a shame we weren't making martinis; they certainly would have been shaken, not stirred!

After what felt like a lifetime, the surface improved somewhat and we made better time, but the highway still enjoyed asserting its special character on us occasionally as we continued south. Finally, we arrived at the end of the gravel and thankfully turned into Red Bay on real asphalt. We didn't actually kiss the ground, but we sure felt like it. We didn't realize it at the time, but this stint of driving in Labrador would be by far the worst of this whole trip. During the rest of our travels the roads would be quite acceptable, although not always perfect. In defence of the Labrador highways, there is so much empty space, so little habitation and so little traffic, that it is difficult to imagine how the roads could be improved without a huge influx of money and labour. Clearly, the government is working on it. Some parts were fine, and we enjoyed driving them, but the gravel sections… they definitely need work.

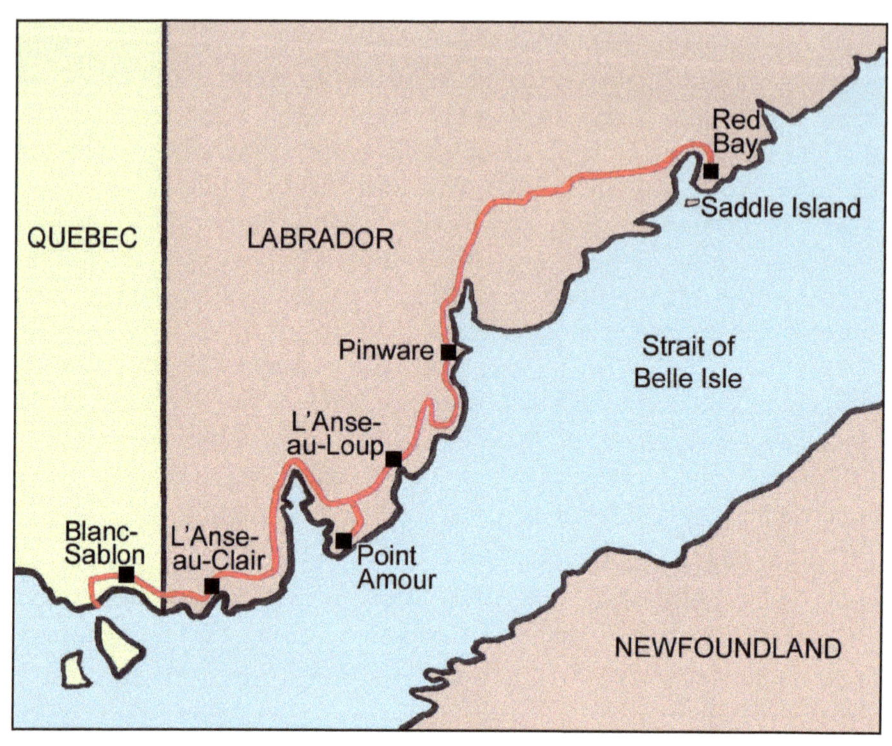

Red Bay to Pinware Provincial Park	32km
Pinware to L'Anse-au-Claire	44km
General tourism	67km
L'Anse-au-Claire to Blanc-Sablon	8km
TOTAL	151km

Chapter Seven
Red Bay to Blanc-Sablon

Now we were finally in Red Bay our first port of call was the Parks Canada office, where we purchased our passes for the two buildings that comprise this site. While we were in the first building we took the opportunity to examine the whaling boat on display, and were amazed at its small size. I can't imagine what it must have been like to be on the open ocean chasing whales in this small craft. Following a quick lunch, we walked down a steep little hill to the main museum building, and were happily surprised to meet our motorcycle friends again. The four of us had left Mary's Harbour together, but our biker friends had quickly left us in their dust, so it was nice to catch up with them here.

This museum, although small by Ottawa standards, is a beautiful place to visit, and we both really enjoyed our experience. The displays are devoted to the 16th century Basque whalers who made this their North American *pied-a-terre* during the hunting season.

The model of the San Juan *in the museum displays gives an idea of the small size of the whaling ships that crossed the Atlantic*

As we visited the displays, reading the interpretive panels and admiring the artifacts, Bob met a few 'old friends'; objects that he had worked on at the Canadian Conservation Institute (CCI). He had treated these precious pieces and helped preserve them, which has allowed them to be displayed for the enjoyment and information of the many visitors. In our meanderings through the museum we found a small notice advertising boat rides to Saddle Island, the actual place where the Basques had lived and worked during the winter whaling season. We had talked about our desire to cross over to Saddle Island, but didn't think it would be possible, so this became a must-see. We rapidly bought our tickets and found the small boat that would ferry us over to the island and back, while allowing us an hour to explore this very interesting place. As we waited for our ride, we chatted with the other couple in the boat, and on arrival we set out to explore the island together.

We were provided with a map of the island showing the various sites of interest where the archaeologists had clearly found evidence of whaling activity. Numbered markers on the ground beside a path that circled the island corresponded to the map, which helped us to imagine what this place must have looked like during that period. There were no actual artifacts on the island, as they were either on display or in storage in the museum (some of which we had actually seen) or reburied.

Much is left to the imagination on Saddle Island. This marker shows the location of the tryworks, where the oil was extracted from whale blubber

Saddle Island is a very peaceful place nowadays. We enjoyed it on a beautifully warm day, with the sea gently washing the shoreline, and the seabirds circling around, providing a very attractive addition to the scenery. It was difficult to imagine how changed it was from over 400 years ago. This must have been a thriving organization, with all the activities and noise associated with whaling and the rendering down of the oil; the sea and the birds simply an unnoticed backdrop.

Red Bay as seen from Saddle Island

As we followed the path we were able to identify areas where the tryworks would have been, thanks to the map. The tryworks was the working area where the whale blubber was boiled to release the oil; close to them the cooperages were found. Here the barrels, brought over in pieces by the whalers, would be reassembled and prepared for the shipping of the oil back to Europe. Again, amid the peace, it was difficult to image the noise and busyness as we walked around this attractive place.

Several sites along the path were identified as the houses where the whalers would have lived. While it was not clear what the population of the island was at any one time, it was clear that this was a reasonable sized community. As with any community of that period, there was a small cemetery, located in one of the most beautiful spots on the island. The business side of whaling was all facing the mainland, while the cemetery was facing out to sea, and thus to the whaler's homeland so many miles away. Many men and boys were buried there, and we were reminded of the countless others who were lost at sea. It was a stark reminder of the harshness of the life the whalers lived and the true human cost of whaling. For those men and boys who survived to return home the rewards were good, which justified for them the risks they were exposed to, but for the others…

The Basque graveyard with individual burials marked with stones

As we walked around the island we chatted with this very interesting couple from Washington DC, who we had met on the boat. Like us, they were retired, but while we enjoy our traveling we always return to our home base. This couple have made their motorhome their only home and over the last few years they have explored much of the USA, South America, parts of Canada and many other places. It was fascinating to learn of their explorations, while thinking that however much we enjoy traveling, it is still a hobby for us, and the return to our 'real' home is always a pleasure. We were discussing our plans for the evening and mentioned we were hoping to stay at Pinware Provincial Park, and specifically campsite 16. This was the recommendation of another chance meeting, where people had suggested to us that number 16 was the best campsite. This couple smiled at this, and informed us they were staying at Pinware and were actually occupying number 16! They agreed it was one of the very best sites in the park, so as we left the island and Red Bay, we joked about racing them to the campsite and stealing their spot. Naturally this didn't happen.

Once we were back on the mainland of Labrador, we headed west and found the campsite at Pinware. In fact, campsite 16 wasn't the only nice spot; number 18 also fronted onto the beach, so we settled there for the night.

The beach at Pinware

Being this close to the beach was a lovely treat, and after supper we walked along the sand, just relaxing, enjoying the sound of the waves and the flocks of gulls and other birds wading in the ocean and flying around. I always admire gulls when they are in their proper environment. They are incredibly beautiful when flying, and when at rest they look so neat and tidy as they stand or walk around; it is such a contrast to seeing them in and around the garbage dumps of the city.

Now Bob had some time to mend our leaky plumbing, and with lots of help from duct tape and zip-ties he managed to cover up the hole in the pipe, which made us both feel happier because we like to feel we respect the beauty of these campgrounds, and we really didn't like having a leaky vehicle. As the day drew to a close, it was brought home to us that our time in Labrador was nearly over. We only had one more day before taking the ferry to St Barbe, Newfoundland, so we planned to make the most of the day and explore the small piece of civilization between Red Bay and Blanc-Sablon, Quebec, before heading over the Strait of Belle Isle to new adventures. This meant an early start in the morning, first to book the ferry for our travel day, and then to explore as much as we could.

While Bob was organizing breakfast he took out the container of his breakfast cereal and got an interesting surprise. We had left Happy Valley–Goose Bay three days ago, and this was our first breakfast in the van since then. We had enjoyed one lovely breakfast in the hotel in Port Hope Simpson, and a second in Battle Harbour. Even with all the joys of the road, it was only at this point we realized the full extent of deprecations of this journey when Bob poured his breakfast cereal into the bowl. All that came out was cereal dust! The last time he had seen it, the cereal was in nice crisp flakes, but now they had been refined and ground into dust! He was not the happiest of campers, but it reminded us how much damage vibration could actually do over time. As we looked at Bob's cereal dust, moistened with milk and now turning to gruel, we actually started to laugh. So he smiled as he ate his dust.

It had rained during the night and it was very foggy and drizzly as we left the campground, but we had a lovely surprise on our way out. A little hare was sitting in the middle of the road, just minding his own business. We slowed down as we drove near to him and, once he noticed we were there, he hopped away into the undergrowth, but not before he had been immortalized by my camera.

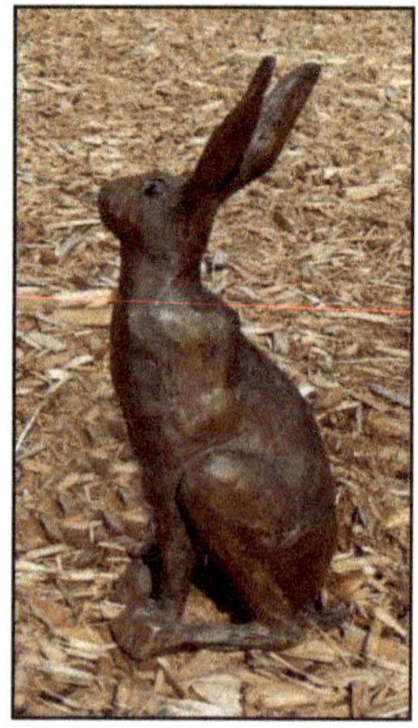

Maybe that's why, almost exactly one year later, while visiting my cousins in the UK, I fell in love with a small sculpture of a hare. After much thought, the hare made the trip back to Canada and now sits quite proudly on our shelves and lets me know how happy he is to be here.

Finally, we were on paved road and although patched, driving was much easier than any of the previous few days. We enjoyed this scenic route as it wound its way around all the little coves, up and down the rather steep headlands along the coast. We located the campsite in L'Anse-au-Clair, booked in for the night and then drove to Blanc-Sablon to book our ferry for early the next day. Surprisingly, we couldn't book our tickets at the terminal itself, but had to phone the booking office from within the ferry terminal! That small chore done we had time to explore this little piece of coast, our final area of Labrador.

We had passed signs for the Labrador Straits Museum, so we made that our first stop. It is a pretty little building with local artifacts collected and displayed by the Women's Institute of the area. Like all such small museums, it held a range of objects, a few of which were really interesting when related to the history of the area.

The Labrador Straits Museum overlooking the Strait of Belle Isle

The most exciting part of the museum turned out to be the staff: Iris Earle-Morency, a native of Labrador, told us about the history of the area and had many stories about the artifacts on display. This made the whole place come alive and helped us understand what it was like living and working on the South Shore in earlier times. The Grade 11 student working with her, Nancy Bolger, was equally fascinated by the stories, and the four of us hoped that one day Iris would have the opportunity to write down all this wonderful information.

Point Amour lighthouse

It was here on the south coast of Labrador we started what turned out to be a tour of many of the lighthouses in the Maritimes. Our visit to Point Amour lighthouse—the tallest one in Newfoundland and

Labrador and the second tallest in Canada—was the first on our unanticipated lighthouse explorations. Point Amour is now a Provincial Historic Site and stands there as a tribute to all the lighthouse keepers and all the lives saved over many years. We climbed up the narrow spiral staircase, with its approximately 200 steps, to the top and looked down at the world from the point of view of the light. Seeing how wide the view was of the Strait of Belle Isle, we began to appreciate the location, especially as it was possible to see some of the less ship-friendly areas in view. The lightbulb itself was quite small, but with the magnification of the Fresnel lenses it can be seen from around 18 nautical miles. As we looked at the land below, we could see our RV, looking like a child's toy parked on a play mat.

The view from the top

During our climb to the light gallery the museum guide described the life and work of one of the original light keepers. He had to check the rotary mechanism and wind up the weights, and keep the original light fueled with oil the whole time, which meant he had to climb these stairs several times a day. In bad and windy weather he would stay up at the top to ensure the light continued burning, as it would often need relighting. If the light had gone out while he was downstairs, there would be enough time for a ship to founder on the rocks before he could get back up those stairs. It is estimated that in his career he ascended and descended 10,000 times. Initially the light was fueled with kerosene, so as well as climbing to the top, he would also need to carry the kerosene up those same stairs twice a day just to refill the tanks. Having climbed the tower just once, I had a much better understanding of the work involved, and came to the conclusion that those early lighthouse keepers must have been extremely strong and very fit.

The view to the west from the top of the lighthouse

The light keeper's family lived in the accommodations at the base of the lighthouse, and this area was set up as it would have been so many years ago. We were seeing it in the summer, but I wondered what it would be like to live there in the winter, with the wind and snow blowing around and through it. The bedrooms had become the display area and included panels on the history of the lighthouse and the events surrounding it, including pictures of several of the ships that had hit the rocks with quite negative results! Around the time the lighthouse was built, Newfoundland and Labrador were not yet part of Canada. Ships from Europe preferred to sail through the Strait of Belle Isle as it shortened the voyage by a couple of days, an important consideration given the costs associated with commerce. While this route may have been faster, it was rockier and more dangerous, so lighthouses were needed to decrease the risk to shipping. In the 1850s the Province of Canada decided to build up to four lighthouses along the Strait, one of which was this one at Point Amour. Interestingly, we learned the name Point Amour is a corruption of Point à Morts, which is altogether more descriptive of this rocky coastline.

Our final tourist stop in Labrador was an Archaic burial site near Point Amour, thought to be about 7,500 years old. It shows as a low mound of rocks, which on closer examination appear to have been placed quite deliberately. This site has been investigated by archaeologists, who uncovered the burial location of a young child wrapped in a shroud of bark or hide and placed in the mound. Red ochre was also present at the site, which has indicated the likelihood of this being the child of a chief, probably of the Dorset-Eskimo group. It is remarkable to think this rather small, and in some ways very modest looking mound, carried so much history of the people of the area so many millennia ago.

The burial mound of a Dorset-Eskimo child; a poignant reminder of the long history of this part of the coast

Finally, on our last afternoon in Labrador, we headed for our campsite at L'Anse-au-Claire. We needed to catch up on all the chores, again. The inside of the van was like a dust bowl from all the roads we had traveled, and the outside of it matched it with the dust and mud spread over it. And, of course, the laundry needed doing, so while this was underway all the bugs that had met their untimely end on our windshield had to be removed. We attacked these chores with a vengeance and finally got everything looking much more presentable.

As we were hard at work, other campers were entering the site. This campground was definitely an overnight spot for most, as well as a home away from home for people working in the area. It was run by the hotel just across the road, and although our guidebook gave it a very low rating, for one night we weren't too concerned. It was also the only convenient campsite in the area, which made it our only realistic choice. When we booked in at the hotel we were given a campsite number, but told that if that site was taken, to just find another, which is exactly what we did. During our mad cleaning session other people were coming in for the night and were looking for numbers that didn't actually exist, so we just passed on the information we had been given: "Find a spot and set up for the night." Though somewhat surprised, the newcomers did just that. In all fairness to the campsite, it was fully serviced with water, hydro and sewer hook-ups, plus a laundry and WiFi coverage, which perfectly suited our needs. Some trailers on the site appeared permanent, and we soon discovered these belonged to employees of projects in the area. The hotels were also full with workers, so it seemed to be sensible that if you had a trailer this was a good place to be.

We spied one couple looking for a tenting spot, so after talking to them briefly, we noticed they were setting up their tent in the adjacent field. We invited them over to share our bottle of wine, bought so long ago (or so it seemed to us) in Goose Bay. It was a delightful evening. He was a visitor from England, she was from Montreal. They had hooked up in Montreal and, using her car, had been all around the Maritimes for the last couple of months. Labrador was their last stop before heading back to Montreal. He did much of his work on-line and could maintain it while on the road, and likewise she was able to monitor her translation business via email. It was a very pleasant interlude, and a lovely way to spent our last night it Labrador.

All too soon the next morning the alarm went off and it was time to pull up stakes and head to the ferry at Blanc Sablon for our early start. Once we were loaded aboard we went straight up on deck to say our last farewells to Labrador as the ferry pulled away from the dock. Then we turned our thoughts to Newfoundland and the further adventures coming our way.

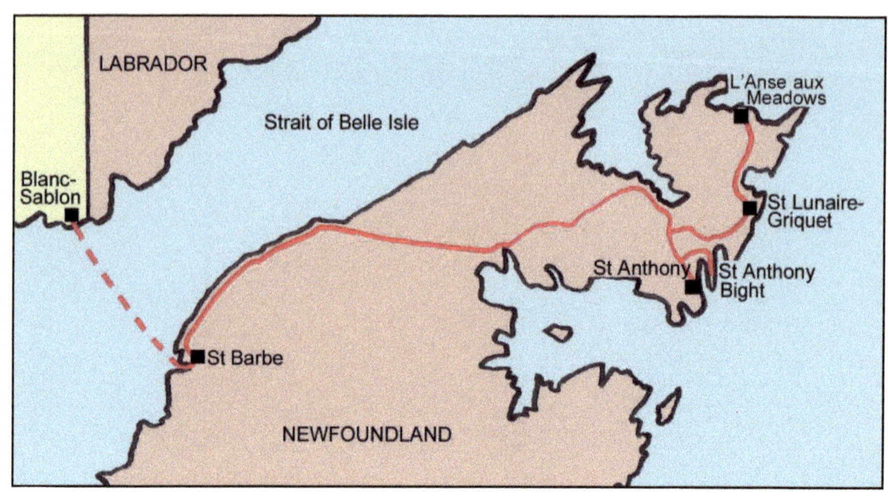

Blanc-Sablon to L'Anse aux Meadows	118km
L'Anse aux Meadows to St Anthony	98km
TOTAL	216km

Chapter Eight
Blanc-Sablon to St Anthony

We were now in Newfoundland, and looking forward to a new kind of experience. In Labrador the very unfamiliar environment and culture became the touchstones of our travels. Visiting the small communities up and down the coastline was a real learning experience for us, and a beginning to our understanding of the issues and challenges of living in this harsh environment. Talk of temperatures of 40 below or more made me shudder just to think about it. Being periodically cut off from the outside world was disturbing to say the least. Now we both feel we have a better understanding of this beautiful yet challenging place and when hearing news of this region, we can better relate to what we hear. It really was a wonderful experience and, the roads aside, I am so glad Bob and I were able to visit this special part of Canada.

Once the ferry docked in St Barbe we headed north towards L'Anse aux Meadows, and our campsite at the Viking RV Park (unique and creative name!) After a brief check in, we made our way to the historic site at L'Anse aux Meadows, the original Viking settlement of the early 11th century. We had always been fascinated by the stories of this out-post on the edge of the 'known world', so when planning this trip it had been on the top of our list. It was a drizzly sort of day, but this didn't deter us as we made our way to the Parks Canada Visitor's Centre to find out as much as possible about this place.

Once in the Centre we were immediately captivated by the incredible display of artifacts from the archaeological site, and spent some time examining them. One of the information boards showed the time it would have taken for a voyage across the North Atlantic. After departing Norway the ship would arrive in Iceland in seven days, then eight days more would bring it to Greenland, and finally, after a further nine days of travel, the ship would likely have reached Vinland; this part of the Newfoundland coast, so called in the Saga of that name. Looking at the estimated time to travel that distance, it made sense the Vikings would 'island-hop', stopping to restock their ships. This was an eye-opener for me; although I knew they were excellent seafarers, I hadn't realized how relatively short the sea-time was between the various settlements. Of course, this assumes good weather, because those voyages would have been longer and more fraught when the North Atlantic was showing its true and rather unpleasant colours.

While at the Centre we took the time to watch a film about the Vikings, or rather Norsemen as they should be known. One thing really struck me: in the movie the narrator spoke about the dispersal and development of humankind from its origins in Africa—moving north first, then dividing east and west—and then only meeting again when the Norse-men encountered the aboriginal population. In essence, they were completing the circle around the world of the development and dispersal of Mankind. This was a real insight for me, and made me think of this whole movement of peoples around the globe in a very different fashion. In addition, the film provided a great deal more information about the Norse and this location, all of which set us up to better understand what we would see when we actually viewed the original site of the settlement, and the recreation of the sod houses as the Norse would have made them.

We followed a boardwalk, which was there to protect the natural environment from visitors while also protecting visitors from all the boggy areas between the archaeological site and the Parks Canada buildings. About halfway along, we came across a sculpture in bronze celebrating the meeting of the Norse and the aboriginal people. It was a wonderful symbolic recreation of the first meeting of two peoples, although the two cultures may not have met face-to-face in quite this way. We do know this particular site was occupied for many thousands of years by the aboriginal peoples, and thus the likelihood of them meeting the Norsemen was very high. The sagas refer to the *skrælings* and the rather negative interactions

they had with the Norse. Other than this brief reference, not much is known about the relationship between these two groups of people.

The recreated site of the buildings was our first stop on this walk. Parks Canada employs docents dressed in contemporary clothing to introduce visitors to the buildings and to describe the activities of the occupants. The sod houses had been designed and built by Parks Canada and furnished according to Icelandic tradition. Since the Norse had come to this area from Iceland, it made a lot of sense to set the scene with information gained from sites there. The houses were quite large and well proportioned, but with no natural light except from the smoke hole in the roof. We learned that these would be the home for up to 20 people; a full boat crew. Suddenly they didn't seem all that big!

The recreated sod houses as the Norse would have seen them

Our next stop was the blacksmith's forge next door, where we had a very informative chat with the blacksmith. This was an amusing meeting; Bob was wearing one of his trumpet-making workshop T-shirts with the picture of a 17th century craftsman and his tools. The blacksmith was fascinated by the shirt, admiring the illustration and checking out all the tools depicted in it. Strangely enough, it was right across the other side of the continent, in Alaska, that this same shirt provoked a conversation. On that occasion, some German tourists who noticed it actually knew the organizer of the workshop in Rostock (see *Points North and West*, p. 153). The smith and Bob segued into a discussion of iron and forging and all sort of other arcane matters. Apparently, the smith had tried to forge iron bloom from bog iron, the raw material the Norse had to use, and he had found it quite difficult, and the yield very low. He and Bob had a long speculation about this, remarking on the tenacity of the early smiths and wondering if, perhaps, their inability to produce enough iron might have contributed to their abandoning the site.

Bob and the blacksmith comparing notes on working bog iron

Having spoken with the docents of the recreated settlement, it was time to examine the real thing. As we looked around we could see a small stream meandering through the area, so with access to both freshwater and a sheltered bay, the location of this settlement started to make sense. The actual mounds where the sod houses had stood over 1000 years ago are easily seen in patterns on the ground; they were clearly house-shaped and indicated where both small and large buildings had been located. It was fairly easy to see where the entrances to the house had been, and where access ways between rooms had been placed. These areas were very well worn and flattened down to a couple of feet below the sides of the houses, and it was possible to imagine people using these doors as they went about their daily work. There were several houses in the area of the settlement, and we both imagined the lives of the original inhabitants and how they had managed in what appeared to us to be such a cold, damp and forbidding place.

The houses are seen as mounds scarcely raised above the surrounding surface. On the left, a dwelling, ship repair and iron forge. Below, a house and a workshop

As we walked slowly back to the Visitor Centre our heads were full of what we had seen. It had been an incredible experience and because of this overload of information and feelings, we were not really sure what we wanted to do next. According to the tourist information we had perused so assiduously, there was another recreated Viking Village in the vicinity. We were somewhat dubious about going to see this–after all, we had just visited the real thing–but we still drove over to it, just in case. When we arrived we realized it was a recreation of what might have happened if the Norse had actually stayed and founded a colony in Newfoundland. We were already filled with such a sense of history that we just preferred to have more time reflect on that experience, rather than see what might have been, so we found a lovely quiet, little café overlooking an attractive inlet, and enjoyed a cup of tea, and a very tasty carrot cake. So, we spent a few peaceful minutes looking out over the sea, and just thinking about all we had seen.

The restful background to our tea and carrot cake

After leaving L'Anse aux Meadows we had a little time to spare, so we drove to St Lunaire-Griquet to visit the Dark Tickle Company. Our travel information reported that this merchant had a selection of local jams, a sure-fire magnet for us. After exploring the gift shop and buying some very intriguing jams made from local berries, a music CD of songs of the area, and a (by now, essential) copy of the *Vinland Sagas* (see Resources, p. 274) we climbed the stairs to the room above the store. Here we found an excellent display detailing the history of the French Shore. We had little idea of the very strong French influence in this area, and learning that visitors from France had lived and worked in this part of Newfound-land for over 400 years was a revelation to us. The display comprised a fascinating collection of pictures, documents and maps, which graphic-ally outlined the political and social history of the area, so after an hour's intensive study we came away a little embarrassed at our previous ignorance of such an important legacy.

Our first day in Newfoundland set the pattern for much of our travels through this incredible island. Its history over the last 500 or so years is extensive and, to my mind, not easily accessible to those of us who have chosen to live in other parts of Canada. It is easy, we find, for people from elsewhere to be dismissive of Newfoundland, falling back on rather tired stereotypes and ignoring the reality we discovered throughout our travels here. We continued our unexpected historical quest the following day, when we made our way to St Anthony and learned more of the story of Dr Wilfred Grenfell and his work in Labrador and this part of Newfoundland. We had some inkling of his presence when we visited the historic sites in North West River, but it took a visit to the Grenfell Historic Properties to really learn the impact of his work (see Resources, p. 274).

Our full introduction to this amazing man was our visit to the Grenfell Interpretation Centre, where we began with a video, using original film footage, which described his life and exploits throughout the area. Wilfred Grenfell was an English physician who came here as a missionary doctor in 1892 and created a health service for the population of Labrador and the north coast of Newfoundland. Over the course of his life he created hospitals, hospital ships, nursing stations, schools and orphanages. He also encouraged industrial development, which helped the people of the region to earn living wages in a productive manner. In short, he was an amazing man who made a profound difference to the quality of life, and one whose legacy still lives on. Although he had a house in St Anthony, he never actually stayed this far north during the true winter months. This was his opportunity to travel south, raising money for his work through lecture tours and sales of his books. During this activity he recruited numerous volunteers who would eagerly travel to Labrador during the summer months to work in the hospitals and missions. As I read *Dear Everybody*, the book we had purchased several weeks ago in North West River, I began to understand how a young New York socialite found herself transported to this part of the world, and ultimately fell in love with the area.

The Interpretation Centre was a mine of wonderful information, and beautifully displayed. After looking around it for over two hours we found it somewhat overwhelming to think of all the good that one person can do when there is the vision, the willpower and the energy to carry it all out. The panels, the original audio clips and the historic photos painted a picture of living on the coast of Labrador; what it must have been like over a hundred years ago, and difference it had made for the inhabitants to have access to medical care on a semi-regular basis. Now all those references to the Grenfell missions, hospitals, nursing stations and hospital ships we had heard about during our travels came into focus. The reverence with which he was held was depicted in a gorgeous stained glass window (see p. 127).

A model of one of Dr Grenfell's first hospital ships

Once we had assimilated all we could from the Interpretation Centre, we crossed the road to the hospital. Grenfell had created this first hospital in St Anthony; over time it has grown and been rebuilt, and is now a modern facility with all the bells and whistles of modern hospitals today. What drew us to this building was the wonderful murals by Jordi Bonet located in the entrance rotunda, and thus experienced by anyone entering through the main doors. These eight murals depict Bonet's vision of the work of Grenfell, starting with the first symbolic tree that representing the one man who came to the coast. In the second panel the trees have multiplied, demonstrating how Grenfell's actions encouraged many other medical professionals to come to the area. The third panel shows the inhabitants before and after his arrival, and the changes in their well-being. In panel number four are seen a fisherman and an abundance of cod, while the fifth panel honours the long history of hunting and trapping. Panel number six shows Bonet's thoughts and impressions of this part of the country, including the full round of the seasons, and incorporates many representations of the land and the sea. The final two panels depict the Innu people of the area, and how they lived. It was these final panels that had the most powerful affect on me. Even so, scanning the whole rotunda you see an incredible and powerful homage to a man who changed the lives of so many people.

While we were busy with this wonderful mural, there were others in the rotunda, waiting to visit family members who were clearly patients in the hospital. It felt a little awkward to be taking photographs in such a location, so I was unable to record these wonderful murals. A small brochure about the murals was available at the reception desk, and with that we were able to content ourselves with the descriptions and small pictures of these wonderful works of art.

Reluctantly, we left the murals and walked to Grenfell's St Anthony residence, which was up a steep trail behind the hospital. This house looked so friendly and welcoming as we approached it from below that I just wanted to walk in and meet the owners! It was a joy to look around and learn even more about this amazing man and his colleagues, and to imagine what his life was like in those far distant days. It was clear from what we saw and read in the house that Grenfell recognized and appreciated the work, support and comfort his wife Anne provided. She had played an important part in encouraging and facilitating all that he did.

One of the rooms in the Grenfell home, furnished as it would have been during his time there

We had spoken briefly with the young girl checking tickets when we first entered the house, so as we left we went to wish her goodbye, only to find her sitting on her desk! Apparently, a small mouse had run across the floor and since she didn't like small animals running around her feet she had taken refuge. So, intrigued, we stayed and chatted with her for a little while as she sat there. She told us that her family were originally of East Indian descent, and had come to St Anthony from Ireland years ago to work at the hospital. Her father is one of the doctors there, and she is planning to follow in his footsteps and study medicine. She is still an Irish citizen, and plans to return to Ireland for her studies.

After wishing this young woman well (and hoping that a fear of mice would not preclude a career in medicine) we left to walk up the hill behind the house, which apparently was a favourite walk for the Grenfells. As we followed the paths we imagined Dr Grenfell and his wife strolling and discussing their work, or perhaps some of the more mundane things in life. We made quite a climb to the top of the hill, coming to a belvedere where, suddenly, the whole of St Anthony opened up below us, including a glimpse of an iceberg grounded in St Anthony Bight, the next inlet along the coast. As we stood there we knew that the Grenfell family had seen similar sights on their many walks to the top. It was a pleasant thing to imagine. Wilfred Grenfell and his wife Anne are buried in this peaceful place; a place where they had spent many hours together.

A brief rest on the walk to the top

The view over St Anthony with the enticing iceberg grounded in St Anthony Bight

Just in case we hadn't had our fill of icebergs, we hurried back down the hill and quickly found our way by road over to St Anthony Bight to see the iceberg we had spotted up close and personal! As we later discovered, St Anthony Bight is quite shallow, so as the currents and tides bring the icebergs into the confined space, they very soon become grounded, and eventually break up into smaller pieces and melt into the sea. While this area could be described as a graveyard for icebergs, it is also a great tourist attraction. As we drove into the little village we noticed a couple of signs advertising iceberg water. It is clear the local entrepreneurs are ready and willing to take advantage of this natural phenomenon by selling the 'real thing' to tourists. We were amused, but didn't buy any.

The stranded iceberg as close as we could get

After admiring the iceberg from every possible angle, we left this small village in a funny way. We had parked the RV on a very steep and narrow hill, and guessed it would pose some challenges when we were ready to leave. We were right! There was no room to turn the vehicle around; after all an RV is a bit bigger than most cars! So Bob got behind the wheel, I stood where he could see me and, gesticulating wildly, much to the amusement of all and sundry, helped him back out, up the hill and round the corner onto the main road of the village. Maybe it wasn't the easiest way to find our way out, but at that point it appeared to be the only way. Judging by the number of onlookers, they probably still talk about it in St Anthony Bight.

Even though it had been a long day of looking and learning, and we were almost 'touristed out', there was one more thing to experience: The Viking Feast. We had seen this advertised in one of our many tourist brochures and unlike the recreated Viking village, this one looked to be simply light-hearted fun, so we went for it. One of the many advantages we have discovered of traveling with an RV is the ability to park your 'house' somewhere and then prepare ourselves for the next engagement. A quick change of clothes and the addition of makeup, and we were ready for an evening out.

The Viking Feast is a very popular event, well managed and a lot of fun. The entrepreneurs who started this have come up with an ideal combination of entertainment, information and good food. The restaurant is built like a sod house and has a large open interior space, although much bigger than those in L'Anse aux Meadows! The tables are long, with wooden benches on either side, and guests are seated as they come. No private tables here! Sitting alongside strangers was a little uncommon to us town folk, and while it created a very different feel to the meal, it didn't take us long to start talking to the other people at our table and getting into the mood of the occasion. Our servers were all dressed as 'Vikings', or so they said. Liberties were taken with the costumes in deference to their various tasks. Our em-cee for the evening was one Captain Hroadsson who was wearing a helmet (although mercifully it was lacking horns) and carrying a sword. He wandered the room around talking and joking with all the guests prior to the feast. Apparently, we would all be participating in a council meeting/law court—an *althing* in Norse practice—so after the meal we were expected to judge cases brought before us. Since, as guests, were part of the council, we were encouraged and expected to bring cases before the council to be judged.

Captain Hroadsson and a serving wench demonstrating the authenticity of the Viking feast and its accoutrements

We were informed by Captain Hroadsson that each table represented a boat crew, identified by name. Then he read out the law and punishments for several crimes and, interestingly, most of them are still featured in today's court system: hitting your wife in public; calling someone a coward; killing someone in daylight; murdering someone secretly at night; stealing from someone; and so on. Things haven't changed much over 1000 years! Neither have people, of course. The judging would be done by boat crew, and when judging guilt or innocence in a specific case, the boat crews would be called by name, and their votes taken. The crew was required to bang on the table, which meant Yes, guilty, while silence meant No, not guilty. If there should be a tie, then Captain Hroadsson, as the Head of Council, would cast the deciding vote. We were admonished to think first and only vote after "thinking wisely" so justice might be served. It all seemed clear and well organized and everyone appeared to be enjoying themselves.

The meal was buffet style, so in order to make it an orderly session each boat crew was called up in turn. Our boat was called up last, because apparently we had not been "thinking wisely!" I am still not clear how that came about, but it really didn't matter. The meal itself was more Newfoundland than Viking, which was rather amusing, and the lack of smoked fish—quite likely one of the Viking staples—suited me just fine. The menu offered salad, Jigg's dinner, roast beef, moose stew, shrimp and rice, cod and cod's tongues, and salmon, all of which were reported to be very good. We had wine with our meal, and wondered whatever might have passed for wine in Vinland a millennium ago. Dessert was a pancake with bake-apple syrup and cream, served right at the table. This was very tasty and the bake-apple syrup was a lovely reminder of all the ones we had so happily consumed in Labrador. We felt very well fed indeed.

The real challenge with the meal lay in eating in a sociable manner, since we were only given a knife and spoon, 'Viking style'. Somehow we managed; the salad was a challenge and eventually fingers came into play! Most fortunate for all us newbie Vikings we were given a good supply of napkins, although I am not sure such niceties would have been available in the 10th and 11th centuries.

The Court Session started soon after dinner with the first case being presented by the resident Vikings. This was quite a serious case. We heard the story of one man killing his father because he had called him a coward. And after he had testified, counter charges were brought before the court by the accused. This set the mood for the rest of the evening, and although I don't remember the outcome of this particular case it was apparently judged 'wisely.' Then it was the turn of the boat crews to bring their own cases forward to the court, and again we all judged them 'wisely'... we hope. Punishments were meted out to fit the crime. One person had to go on bended knee and tell his mother-in-law he loved her; another had to dance a jig; a couple of freeloaders (teenage kids on vacation) were tied together for a while (30 seconds) because they had been too shy to defend themselves; and so on. It was a lot of fun and by the end of it everyone was laughing and cheering the actors and the guests who had stepped forward with their silly, or perhaps not so silly, complaints.

At the end of the evening a number of the guests requested they be Screeched-in, which finished the evening in grand style. This ceremony was a little different from the one we had enjoyed in Battle Harbour. There we had only to dress up, while these poor souls had to stand in ice water while they kissed the cod and recited a very silly rhyme. Finally, they had to drink the shot of Screech, or apple juice for the underage crew. It was a lot of fun and by the end of it the whole restaurant appeared to be in great spirits.

On a more serious note, during the evening we also had an opportunity to talk seriously with Captain Hroadsson, who was evidently not simply an actor playing a part. He clearly knew the sagas and the history of the area very well, which resulted in a really deep and interesting discussion. At this point it was clear that I needed to start reading my copy of the *Vinland Sagas* in order to understand more of the history of this period. I realized, of course, that these tales were likely revised as they had been retold over many generations, until finally being written down centuries later. Over the course of the next few weeks I did read and enjoy the *Sagas* in translation. The stories are well worth reading and thinking about, especially where they relate to this remote part of the world.

So ended our sojourn in St Anthony. As we drove back to Triple Falls RV Park—a second campsite we had chosen because it was on our route out the next day—we talked about all we had seen and experienced. We were quite excited but a little nervous as we thought about our next port of call, Conche. This little village is at the end of a 20km gravel road, which gave us some concern because we had seen enough of gravel for a lifetime. The big draw, however, was a description of a tapestry embroidered by the ladies of the village, in the style of the Bayeux Tapestry and of the same length as that very famous piece. We just hoped the visit would be worth the drive.

LOVIS
WILFRED
GREN-

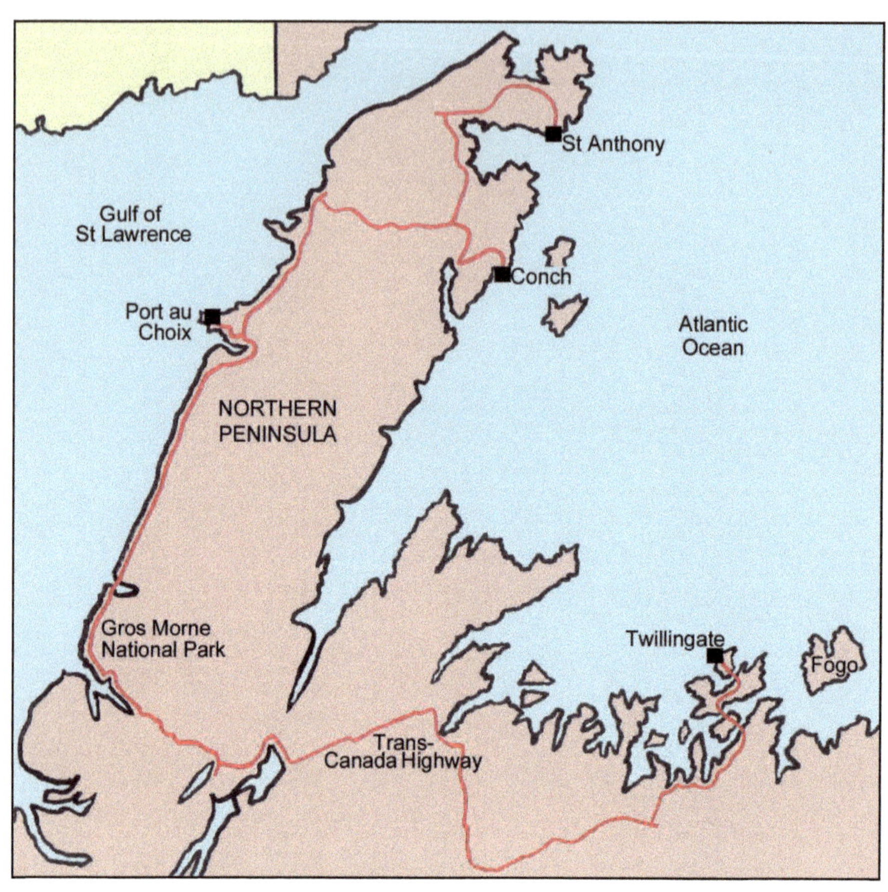

St Anthony to Port au Choix	373km
Port au Choix to Gros Morne	176km
Gros Morne to Twillingate	440km
TOTAL	989km

Chapter Nine
St Anthony to Twillingate

Early the next morning we headed towards the French Shore and the little village of Conche. The weather was not promising; it was raining, and given our experiences with mud and gravel roads we were a little concerned. However, our curiosity about the French Shore Tapestry was such that we were prepared to take whatever the road threw at us. After all, it was only 20km! We had originally planned to continue to Gros Morne and stay there that night, but as we made our way to Conche we began to realize this was an unrealistic expectation, so we relaxed and just enjoyed the drive to the French Shore. Happily, the gravel road was in reasonable condition, so we were able to travel quite comfortably. We turned off the road and into this charming village and soon found the Conche Interpretation Centre. As a side note, the signage was not very good, so initially we drove right past the building before realizing where we needed to be.

The first impression of Conche as you approach from the road

The Centre was a joy to visit. The staff were very friendly and helpful and the two display areas were extremely well laid out. The first area describes the history of this little coastal hamlet, with many pictures and artifacts with accompanying panels on display. These helped enhance our knowledge of the French Shore, which had first been whetted at St Lunaire-Griquet.

Overall view of the historical section of the Conche Interpretation Centre

We had concentrated on this introductory area first, almost as if we wanted a slow lead-up to the big experience. Finally it was time to enter the room housing the French Shore Tapestry. At this point we had no idea quite what to expect. We were both excited and apprehensive to see it and were wondering whether or not it justified our somewhat circuitous deviation from the road to Gros Morne. We were rewarded with an incredible sight. It quite took our breath away. In theory, we knew the Tapestry was 222ft long and that it replicated the Bayeux Tapestry in dimensions, but to see it set up on its wooden supports as it wove around the room was absolutely stunning. For a few moments we just stood and stared at this wonderful sight. We understood, from all the information we had read, that the embroiderers had used the same techniques and stitches used in the Bayeux Tapestry nearly 1,000 years ago—couching and stem stitch, and a few other specialized stitches—but our first magical impression was of the high quality and extremely fine details. Prior to entering the room, we had been told by the staff of the incredible amount of research that needed to be done before the various panels could even be designed. And we were told about Jean Claude Roy, the French artist who was selected to create the designs for this fantastic work, and what a job he had done. As well, we read the biographies of the nine local embroiderers who were commissioned to produce the entire tapestry over 24 months. The inhabitants of this delightful village had soon got to know Jean Claude Roy quite well as he stayed in this little village during the whole process.

An example of the fine tapestry work in another work by the Conch embroiderers

Unfortunately, photography of the French Shore Tapestry was not permitted, but images can be seen on the Conche Interpretation Centre website (see Resources, p. 274).

The Tapestry outlines the entire history of the French Shore, using framed scenes of the various epochs along its length, with extra ornamental bands at top and bottom. There are explanatory panels beneath each scene detailing and describing the depictions. These scenes cover all the major mileposts in the history of the area, showing such periods as the arrival of the Vikings and the meeting of French sailors and native people. The Basque whalers are there too, as is the Treaty of Utrecht, with Queen Anne and Louis XIV depicted in all their glory. The Grenfell Nursing Station is represented, as well as the impact of World War II and the plane crash that occurred outside the local school. But this description can only skim the surface of all the scenes represented along the 222-foot length of the French Shore Tapestry. This is a wonderful work of art that would grace any great museum or art gallery anywhere in the world, yet we found it here in a small village of Newfoundland.

We spent at least two hours poring over the Tapestry, absorbing the information on the labels, marveling at the intricacy, detail and skill, and were totally enthralled. I would happily go back there to spend more time just examining it and enjoying the vivid colours, the incredible pictorial skills of Jean Claude Roy, and the skill and patience of the nine embroiderers. Having seen this wonderful piece of work, Bob and I both agreed it should be visited by as many people as possible, and we were surprised that none of the many museums in Newfoundland have been able to display this amazing piece of work. We were saddened that so few people even know about the French Shore Tapestry, and we sincerely hope it can be better advertised so tourists can see it in its proper setting. Perhaps with increased advertising and a well-paved road, more tourists would be tempted to come to Conche to enjoy this wonderful piece of artistry?

As a side note, we did wonder why the tapestry depicted so many 'penguins' in various areas in the work. It was only later we realized these 'penguins' were in fact images of the great auk, which used to flourish in this area, and was sadly hunted to extinction (see p. 144).

We also spent time with the Centre's administrator discussing increased publicity for the Tapestry. She indicated that there were many difficulties in this, and wished more could be done. There is an ongoing injunction on photographing the tapestry, and at the present time virtually no pictures of it are available, and there are no postcards for sale as mementos of the visit. The administrator voiced her concerns about the state of the road, and hoped at some time it could be paved, thus creating an easy way for tourists to visit this very pretty town and see this remarkable work. While the road was much easier to drive than many we had been on, we later learned from friends who had heard about the Tapestry, the fact it was a gravel road had deterred them from the drive. They missed a treat.

In the basement of the Centre there is a workshop where other pieces are being produced by embroiderers. These new panels depict scenes from the Treaty of Utrecht and its impact on the history of the French Shore. This is intended to be a traveling exhibition and will undoubtedly raise the profile of Conche, and perhaps encourage more people to visit. It was great to see the work in progress and to discuss the techniques in some detail. And here it was a pleasure to take pictures of the work.

Fishing processes depicted in tapestry

We were now tired and hungry, and feeling a little overwhelmed. (It is surprising how much an aesthetic experience can cost in energy.) To wind down, we found the local teashop and had a very lovely lunch of delicious beef soup. It was like a Jigg's dinner in a bowl, and was complemented with a very chunky toasted sandwich. We were the only customers at first; it was a very rainy day and not many tourists had showed up, so shortly after we arrived we were amused to see the owner's husband come by, bringing her laptop to help relieve her boredom. This appeared to be the catalyst that brought other customers to the teashop, and so the computer was neglected as business picked up.

The rain had set in for the day, and as we headed out of Conche we wondered where we would stop for the night. By now, making our way as far as Gros Morne didn't seem feasible, but Port au Choix seemed to be a good alternative, so after an afternoon's drive we located the town's campground right on the seashore. This simple and interesting spot is run by the local Lion's Club, and it has all the basic facilities one could need. We imagined it would be a lovely place to stay, when and if the rain ever stopped, but this didn't happen the whole time we were there. The rain and wind continued all night, with gusts that made our poor van shake and protest as it was hit sideways-on by the force of the wind. We were happy to be inside the vehicle and dry, and not listening to rain pattering on a tent, as we had done so many times in our camping life. That would not have been a pleasant experience, and would likely have sent us in search of a hotel!

Next morning was perfect—wet, windy and cold—to spend some time in a warm museum; the Port au Choix National Historic site run by Parks Canada. We understood from our readings that this area had been populated for thousands of years and had been home to many different peoples over this period. The archaeologists who had explored this area had established that the four main occupants were the Maritime Archaic Indian, Dorset and Groswater Paleoeskimo, and the Beothuk. The site staff were very knowledgeable on the archaeology and history of the region, and were happy to share as much as possible with us. They recommended we watch the introductory movie first, which would give us an overview of the region's history and topography. It was a very helpful production, and a good guide to the displays in the museum itself. We looked around the exhibits, finding some really fine artifacts from the four different settlement periods in this area, all laid out chronologically, which helped us to understand the movement of these peoples. The craftsmanship of the tools was incredible; some of the stone knapping was extremely fine and intricate. Quite phenomenal when one considered how basic were the tools these peoples had to work with. Having enjoyed our visit, we took the time to buy a pass to all Parks Canada sites in the nation, which, from previous experience, we knew we would use throughout the rest of our travels.

The displays in the Port au Choix National Historic site

There are a number of walks that can be taken around the Centre, leading the visitor through the archaeological sites of early settlements, as well as the variety of landscapes encountered in this area. However, the pouring rain, dashed into our faces almost horizontally by the near gale-force wind, made any outside exploration less than conducive. We opted not to take a walk; that is for another visit sometime in the future.

It was time to start our delayed visit to Gros Morne, our destination for the night. As we drove further south we were able to escape the rain and begin to enjoy the drive. We stopped for lunch at a hotel restaurant in Cow Bay where, much to our surprise and amusement, I met one of my colleagues from my aqua-fit class, so far away in Ottawa. She and a friend were traveling around Newfoundland and, unlike us, were close to the end of their journey. We talked about our mutual travels and were able to share ideas for further explorations in the time we both had left. It always seems odd to meet friends and acquaintances from home, when traveling so far away from our home.

Finally, we arrived in Gros Morne. What can we say about Gros Morne that has not been said before? We kept stopping along the road just to take pictures and admire the scenery of this stunning place, rainless and enhanced by glorious sunshine and wonderful views.

Stunning views of the mountains, still shrouded in mist

We stopped to visit the lighthouse at Lobster Cove Head (left), and listened briefly to a Parks Canada interpreter describing a shipwreck and rescue that had occurred in the area. We didn't hear the whole story, but what we did hear told us she was a great story teller. While we were walking back to the vehicle, we came across a happy young couple coming to the lighthouse to have their wedding pictures taken. After congratulating them, we both thought it was a wonderful and, to us folks from Ontario, a very different place for wedding pictures. They were just luckily they hadn't wanted to be photographed in Port au Choix the previous day!

While were wondering where to stay for the night, we took a walk to view Berry Hill Pond. This was classified as an easy walk, which fitted us quite beautifully, so we climbed up a hill to an overlook that gave us a view of this very round pond. The view was something to behold, and from the overlook we could see Gros Morne itself, a backdrop rising to 806m.

The view from the (modest) height of our walk

From where we were standing we thought we could just make out the trail up the mountain. The trail is about 16km and takes all day to get up and down (at least, for folks like us). While it might have been interesting to do, we really didn't feel it suited our needs at this point. Instead, we traveled that road vicariously by speaking to a fellow camper who had walked up and down the mountain and had really enjoyed the experience. As we stood staring at Berry Hill Pond we noticed from on high that there was a campsite attached to it, as well as another short trail around the pond, which we thought would be a nice post-supper walk. That was the deciding factor, and very quickly we descended the hill, drove back to the park gate and booked into the campsite for the night. Our post-supper exploration of the trail was quickly cut short as the thunderstorms and rain we had so happily left behind in Port au Choix caught up with us. A practical decision was quickly made; this walk would have to wait for the next day.

Views along the Berry Hill and Pond trails

The next morning the weather had cleared, so before leaving this lovely spot we decided to check out Berry Hill Pond. Right at beginning of the trail we noticed a great deal of devastation; trees of every size and description, fallen and broken in various directions. Grasses and bushes were already growing up around the trees, which indicated this damage had occurred several years ago. It must have been quite something to see; maybe it was a tornado or some other critical weather event, but we were never able to find out. The circuit around the pond was very pleasant, with beaver lodges, nesting birds and glimpses of the water to feast our eyes and camera on. This was a perfect start to the day.

On leaving the campsite we thought it a good idea to stop at the Information/Interpretive Centre, although it might have been a better idea to do this the day before. Our first impression was the crowding in such a small space, and it seemed to us the staff were merely there to direct traffic! I am sure that on a quieter day we would have been able to question the staff, but on this day it was impossible. As we checked out the displays it became clear that in all our wanderings we had gathered most of the information offered, so we moved on to the gift shop. Here we had a lovely conversation with the gift shop lady, who obviously treasured her encounters with visitors and made much of our presence. I bought a muffin and bread cookbook, full of recipes from the region, and have since made some of them very successfully. The visit to the Centre marked our departure from the Park and we headed toward Twillingate, where we hoped to spend a couple of days. It would have been nice to spend more time in Gros Morne, but our rather ambitious travel plans would not allow it. That will have to wait for another year. This seems to an ongoing theme throughout our travels in Newfoundland. There is so much to see, and even though we allowed a month to enjoy everything about this fascinating place, we were learning very rapidly, this was just not enough time, and further visits would be necessary.

Our last view of Gros Morne as we left the park

The road out of Gros Morne is very scenic. Wonderful vistas would open up around each bend as we rose and descended through the hills and mountains. Each corner offered a new and open vista. We stopped several times to take pictures, but truly the photos I took barely capture the beauty of it all. So in the end I gave up and just enjoyed the scenery as Bob drove. Below is a picture that sort of proves the point.

The weather continued cloudy, which didn't help our pictures

Our road finally joined the Trans-Canada Highway and, as we turned onto it we realized that over our last 26 years of tourism we have traveled almost its entire length. The only piece still to drive is on Vancouver Island, the highway from the ferry terminal at Sidney to Tofino on the west coast. Our youngest son rode his bike from Vancouver to Tofino with a group of friends, so he has done that piece for us, but even with this family help, driving that piece is still on our bucket list.

For the first time in a couple of weeks we could enjoy the pleasure of driving a fast highway, so different from the many small roads we had been on. But, while fast, it was not the most interesting road to drive, with forests of black spruce, the monotony broken only by the occasional unidentified deciduous grove. As along any highway, the occasional gas station and cluster of restaurants and services would appear and then disappear behind us. It was the perfect road to listen to music, switch to cruise control (once we remembered we had it) and just cruise down the road. We continued to encounter intermittent rain, not an unexpected occurrence here in Newfoundland, and in this case, not too challenging. As we turned off the Trans-Canada and headed north towards Twillingate, the scenery became much more interesting. The roads became narrower, there were glimpses of the sea, charming little villages, and several harbours. We were still 'enjoying' the Black Spruce, but even this was decreasing as we made our way to our own 'harbour' for the night.

We arrived in the charming town of Twillingate and quickly found the town campground with its friendly owner. He was very helpful and had lots of ideas for activities that he thought might be of interest to us. He also had some lovely fresh cod for sale, and we happily purchased it with the view to making a pot of chowder with some, and pan-frying the rest. This campground was not one of the more fancy resorts, but it had all the amenities we needed, with the added joy of being able to look out of our vehicle and see a wonderful view of the headland and sea. It was time to remember all we had so far seen and done, and to plan our time in this quintessential location which carries such resonance in the Canadian psyche.

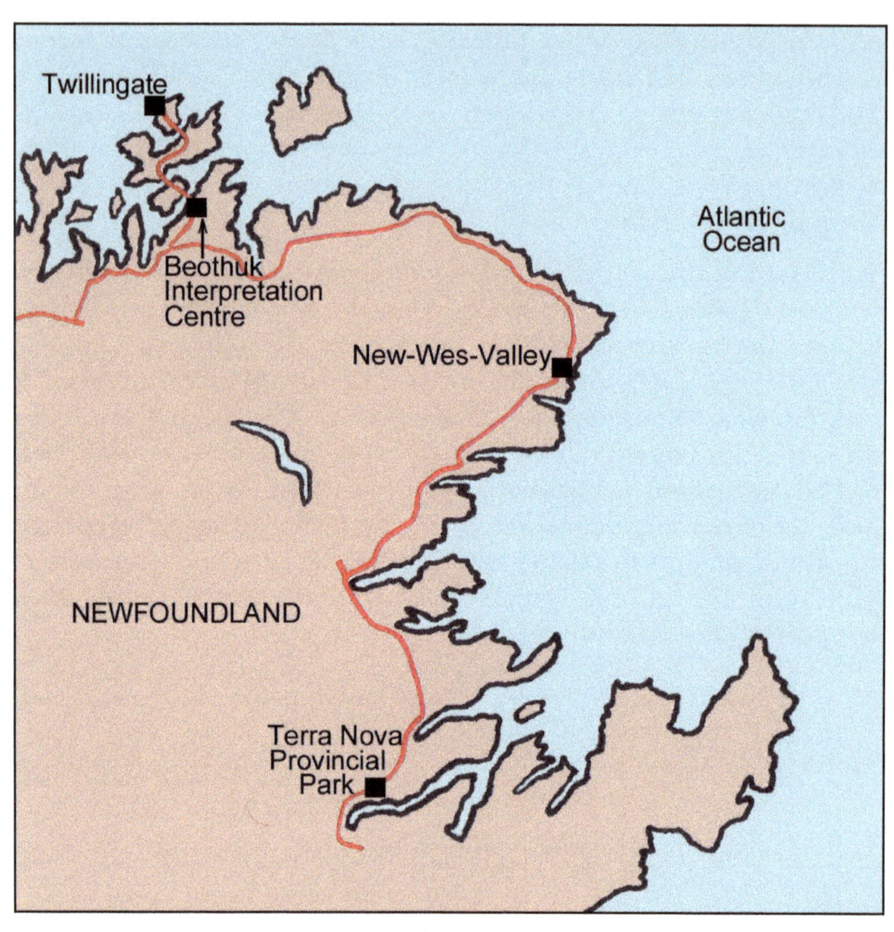

Travel around Twillingate	30km
Twillingate to Terra Nova	294km
TOTAL	324km

Chapter Ten

Twillingate to Terra Nova

We were getting used to the changeable weather in Newfoundland! So far we had passed through cool, damp, wind and rain, and finally into sun. Then Twillingate added fog into the mix. We woke to a cold and foggy day, which led quite naturally to a visit to the Long Point Lighthouse to hear the foghorn. The drive to the end of the point was a bit of a challenge along a narrow and twisting road in the fog. Not that the road itself was bad—it was actually quite good—but since the fog obscured how nice it was, it proved to be a slow drive. As we neared the point we could hear the foghorn clearly, but we could only see the lighthouse when up-close and personal with it! It was cold and windy, and looking down through the strands of fog at the rocks around the base of the lighthouse, I could imagine all too clearly the fate of ships without this warning horn.

Walking around Long Point was an eerie experience; visibility was severely limited and with the wind, the shifting fog and the mournful sound of the foghorn, the feeling of almost being in an alien environment became overwhelming. We were glad when we left and make our way to a down-to-earth winery.

Long Point light trying not to be seen by tourists

The Auk Winery is named after the great auk, which was hunted to near extinction here. The last pair of nesting great auks met their end in Iceland in June of 1844. This bird is a member of the penguin family and it certainly looks like that in contemporary artworks. I remembered wondering about the 'penguins' I had noticed embroidered on the French Shore Tapestry at Conche, and now discovered that what was depicted was actually the great auk. Now it made sense. So, although people often wrongly assume that penguins inhabit the North, one member of the family certainly used to.

Naturally, we had to take a tour of the winery (right). After all, we have visited many grape wineries, and wondered how different this one would be. It turned out that, while the actual wine-making process is very similar, the big difference is in the collection of the berries and fruits. There are no vineyards or berry farms here in Twillingate, but instead local collectors pick the majority of the berries and fruits in the wild and bring them to the winery for processing. These local fruits strawberries, raspberries, blueberries, cloudberries, bakeapple berries, blackcurrants and partridge berries, and wild rhubarb is used as well. This is quite different from the cultivated vineyards we have seen in other places. While the production process is the same, unlike grape wineries, the vintner recommends only keeping these fruit wines for a short time, as they do not have the aging properties of grape wines. Apparently, they will deteriorate after four years or less, unlike some red wines that may be aged for 10 or more years before drinking. The fruit wines are light in colour and flavour, and the sommelier advised us to drink them very cool; much cooler than the various varieties of white wines. This winery has grown and prospered over the last few years, receives orders from customers across Canada, and ships boxes of wine across the country for the very modest delivery fee of $10.00 per case. Something to think about for the future.

The all-important tasting was next. We had a wide choice: a large array of bottles on the tasting table representative of most of the wines produced here. In some cases the vintner had blended grape juice with the local fruit, while others were blends of just the fruits, creating a wide range of flavours and colours. We were curious to learn where the grapes were grown, as the climate Twillingate is not suited to growing them, and were told they were imported as juice. With such a variety and number wines to sample, we needed to be sensible; after all, we were manoeuvring a large vehicle around narrow roads in fog.

Our biggest challenge with this tasting was the contrast between these fruit wines and the grape wines we normally enjoy. The flavour is very different, understandably so, and initially we were not sure what to make of any of them. But as we prepared ourselves for the different flavours, we found some we really enjoyed, but others not so much; very similar to wine tastings we have done elsewhere. A couple of the wines had been made with iceberg water, but really the only perceptible difference comes from the *idea* of the water coming from icebergs; and, of course, the price. Ultimately, we bought a few small bottles and over the next few weeks enjoyed them with our meals.

After our busy morning we found an attractive park overlooking an inlet, and enjoyed our lunch while relaxing with this peaceful, albeit foggy, scene. The cold and damp weather had set in for the day, which turned out to be a positive experience for us. We needed indoor experiences, and so we found the local museum.

The Twillingate Museum (left) is a charming place, well laid out and with lots of local information. It is housed in the former Anglican Rectory, which was built in 1915. We had always wondered about the name of this attractive place, so we were happy to learn its origin: it seems Twillingate is a corruption of the Breton place name

Toulinquet. According to local history, the French fishing fleet were using this area in the late 17th century as a temporary harbour for their ships, as well as a safe haven if needed. The Bretons named it Toulinquet because the islands in the area reminded them of the islands near Brest, on the north coast of France. When the first settlers arrived a few years later the name became anglicized to Twillingate, and has remained that way.

As we explored the museum we came across the story of the Nightingale of the North. At first glance, we expected to read about a local family who had imported a nightingale from faraway places, but that was not the case, and the true story was even better. It was like a fairy tale, but in this case a true one. Miss Georgina Stirling, who was born in 1867, developed a beautiful soprano voice.

The display case featuring Miss Georgina Stirling, the Nightingale of the North

Georgina's ability was recognized very early, so in the 1880s she was sent to Italy for operatic training. Her debut was at La Scala Opera House in Milan, receiving excellent reviews. Following this, she toured Europe and North America with great critical acclaim. At that time, using one's own name was not an option; she needed a stage name with a European flavour, so she became known as Marie Toulinguet, as a reminder of her origins. It is amusing to think that Georgina used the original name of the town, thus completing the circle from Toulinquet to Twillingate, and now back almost to Toulinquet. After performing for several years in Europe, Marie's voice failed her and by 1901 she was residing in England with her sisters, and no longer singing. After World War I she returned to Twillingate, where she stayed until her death in 1935. This was a wonderful story and completely new to us.

After enjoying Georgina's story, we continued around the museum and read the histories of the many important families in the area, and the positions they held; magistrates, churchmen, doctors and nurses. These displays really made this small town come alive, while demonstrating both the economic and social importance of this region. It was clear that in its heyday, Twillingate was not just a small fishing port, but a vibrant centre of the community.

The museum's front door faces St Andrew's Church, just across the parking lot, so after visiting the museum, we walked over. This beautiful building, built in 1840, is surprisingly large, and in its early days it would have been filled for every service.

St Andrew's Church is surprisingly spacious and equipped with a very fine organ

Nowadays, the congregation is much smaller, and the upper gallery remains closed. On entering the building we noticed the overall sense of simplicity and warmth. The interior woodwork was beautifully done, with restful patterns made by graining the wood in specific areas. Likewise, the stained-glass work was very simple and beautifully done and added to the ambiance of this calming place. Bob spent some time examining the organ, which had been erected in 1895, and appreciating its workmanship. After wandering around and just enjoying this calming place, we spoke to a couple of ladies at the entrance desk to learn some of the history.

One of the stained glass windows

Originally, this was the only church in the area, so everyone came here for services no matter what their denomination. As the population grew, so did the number of churches, which ultimately led to a decline in this particular congregation. However, this was soon counterbalanced as the population of Twillingate increased, and until fairly recent times the church has been a very active and important part of the community. But it seems this charming place is suffering the fate of so many churches today, as populations become more secularized. One hopes the present congregation will be able maintain this lovely structure over the coming years.

After this delightful interlude we headed back to the camper with enough time to prepare for the evening's entertainment. We had enjoyed the Viking Feast in St Anthony, so when we noticed an advertisement for a Dinner Theatre we thought it would be fun to see what was on offer. No sooner said than done! We had bought our tickets at Community Centre that morning, ordered our dinner, and planned for the evening. Now the time had come, and we found our way back to the Community Centre, ready to relax and enjoy a pleasant evening. The Dinner Theatre is held every evening except Sunday, with two additional lunchtime sessions, so this is a really hardworking group of actors. The Community Centre was a large building with a good sized parking lot, which was quite full by the time we arrived. Having never attended a dinner theatre we did not know what to expect. As with the Viking Feast, we were seated at a table with a group of other people, and naturally started chatting and discussing our travels. Then, on looking around, we were surprised to spot our friends Linda and Mike, last seen in Port Hope Simpson, Labrador. There they were, sitting at the table next to us! We promised to take some time catching on with all things.

We really enjoyed our supper, especially me because I didn't have to cook it. We started with a very tasty soup, followed by either cod or chicken (as ordered earlier) completed by a very good carrot cake with tea or coffee. Once the crowd had been well fed, the servers turned into actors, reminiscent of our experience in St Anthony. This time there were no cases to judge, but rather some very amusing and very topical skits—Rob Ford, Mayor of Toronto, featured prominently in one of these—interspersed with songs and music of the area. Many of the skits were very much based in that self-deprecating humour so common in Newfoundland, and were very funny. It was clear from the reaction of the large crowd—and especially a number of local people—that the topical context of several of the skits was recognized and enjoyed. The skill of the players in making those commentaries relevant to the audience was impressive. The performers encouraged the audience to participate in the songs, which was appreciated and fully supported by all, and many of those old favourites were played and sung by the performers and their guests. The show itself lasted about an hour and half, and was very worthwhile seeing. Unfortunately, due to the large crowd the pictures taken of this very enjoyable evening, show more of the audience than the players, so they remain relegated to the back of the cupboard!

Out in the parking lot we spent some time catching with Linda and Mike. We compared notes about our adventures and travails since we last met, and shared our horrors of the road. Like ours, that last gravel road in Labrador had left its mark on their vehicle. In the upper corner of the camper, right at the back, a stone or rock had punctured a hole through the exterior wall. Fortunately for them their RV was painted in a similar colour to duct tape! So after they applied that wonderful handyman's friend their little hole was hardly visible. However, they planned to have it properly fixed at the end of their travels. Much to our embarrassment, when we had arrived at the campground the previous evening we hadn't really noticed the camper right next to us!

They recognised our vehicle, and had been looking out for us! After chatting for quite a while in the cool night air, we all headed back to the campground. We were the last ones left in the parking lot of the Community Centre; even the staff had gone home! As we followed their camper back to the campground along the narrow and twisting roads of Twillingate, it was a reminder to us of how the drivers of other vehicles must feel when they follow us.

During the evening meal and entertainment we had chatted to a couple from St John's, telling them about our plans to visit Fogo Island the next day. They had serious doubts about the weather, especially the high risk of fog, which would hinder our sightseeing. They were proved right; it was still foggy and somewhat chilly when we woke up, so being the flexible travelers we are, we looked for other options for the day. Household chores fitted the bill, unfortunately. Not the most fun! We also spent some time with Linda and Michael, and we both felt sure we would meet them again during our travels. (Next time we would make sure to recognize their vehicle!) Once the chores were completed we left Twillingate, heading towards Terra Nova National Park via the coast road. As we drove south we came across road signs for Morton's Harbour and Fogo, and they gave me a better understanding of the lyrics of *I'se the B'y*. We had heard this old favourite again during the dinner theatre and had joined in the chorus along with the rest of the audience. Now, with the proximity of Morton's Harbour and Fogo, we understood what "all around the circle" really meant (see p. 275).

Fog over Twillingate harbour meant that a visit to Fogo would probably not go well

We had been told of an interpretation centre focused on the Beothuk people, so we stopped there on our way back to the mainland. Our immediate impression of the Beothuk Interpretation Centre was how beautifully laid out it was. On walking up a short flight of wooden stairs to the building, we appreciated the ambience of this peaceful place. The Centre is not that large, but it houses some wonderful artifacts; everything from flint and stone tools, basketry, and fishnets with hooks made of bone, to earthenware bowls with residues of ochre. Ochre, a natural earth pigment, was important to the Beothuk and was used in many of their ceremonies. It seems that this red ochre paste, which was used to cover their bodies, may have created the mythology of the Red Indian in the eyes of European explorers. In addition to the artifacts, there was a life size panorama of a Beothuk family setting out with their canoe. The whole experience was quite an eye-opener for me, as I had no real knowledge of these people and the civilization they had created in this part of the world.

The Beothuk Interpretation Centre, reminiscent of two longhouses side-by-side

Interpretive panels described the lives of this people and, of course, their demise. It was rather upsetting to realize how the influx of European settlers had caused the extinction of the Beothuk in the 1820s. The last survivor, Shanawdithit, died of tuberculosis in 1829, and it was she who spoke about her people and was able to describe some of their practices. About 150 years after her death an archaeologist from Memorial University was searching for evidence of these people, and eventually came across exactly the right topographical location for a Beothuk settlement; a large flat plain with an embankment protecting it from the sea, a stream running nearby, which would allow people to take advantage of the smelt run in the spring. As he started closer examination of the area he found evidence of habitation in the form of dug-out areas, where the tepees would have been placed and supported by low earth walls.

The remains of the low walls were not as distinctive as those of the Norse settlement we had seen at L'Anse aux Meadows; they more subtle and less visible, hence the markers

After some years of excavation the archaeologists discovered artifacts dating from between 1640 and the 1750s, from which they were able to reconstruct some of the history of these people. It was clear from the evidence that they had a close dependence on the sea and all its food, which meant that as they were pushed inland, starvation and European diseases would likely have been factors in their extinction.

So, after learning this history, we followed a trail to the actual archaeological site some distance away, where we could view the mounds where the tepees would have sat. This location is now considered a spiritual place by the native population, and looking over the scenery I could totally understand and respect those feelings. As we made our way there we appreciated why this would have been a great place to live for a culture based on the coasts and rivers. The little stream running through the settlement was quite full and fast, and no doubt provided fresh water as well as fish; the site was high and protected from the sea, and the trees around it would have helped tame the wind. It really was an ideal place for a permanent camp. The archaeologists had identified the location of eleven building sites, four of which have been examined so far, so there is still much to learn about this group of people.

The stream that passed beside the campsite, and its outlet to the sea

Along the footpath to the site we noticed that many of the plants local to the area had been labeled and identified, and since it was berry season we could see at first hand the many food sources the Beothuk had access to. There were several interpretive panels snuggled into the bushes on the side of the path, giving more information on the people and the area. Closer to the actual site we came across a life-sized statue called *The Spirit of the Beothuk* (below), which was installed in their honour and remembrance. After lingering a while at the archaeological site we headed back to the Information Centre, appreciating anew just how much impact the 'discovery' of the New World had made on the people of this land.

We left the Beothuk Interpretation Centre with much food for thought, and headed towards Terra Nova National Park. Rather than take the direct route inland, we decided to take the longer coastal and thus more scenic road, which turned out to be an interesting choice. We thought from the map that the road skirted the sea for much of the distance, but this assumption proved to be not quite accurate. The road took us slightly inland, so there were few opportunities to drive along the coastline. In reality it took us through scrubland with stones and rocks scattered around, alternating with wonderful vistas of the hills, headlands and coves, with the occasional settlement thrown in for good measure.

As we made our way along the road, we saw the many small spur roads leading into the coastal villages, but we had not allowed enough time to explore these charming places. Occasionally we drove by some little houses clustered around bays and coves, which made us realize just what lovely spots we were missing. The scrubland and rocks were a constant along the road. As we drove along we could see the rocks just sitting in ponds, on the scrubland, and of course in the sea. It was a landscape that was different from anything we had seen before and reminded us of children just playing with stones, and throwing them around a very large part of the countryside. However, these rocks would have needed to be thrown by some very big children! Fortunately the road itself was clear of rocks, which made driving much easier than in some of our previous experiences.

Fog was also an ongoing friend, and as we drove in and out of the mini fog banks, we developed a feeling for what it must be like to live on this coast. It increased our respect for the hardiness of the people who settled in these areas so many years ago. But there was charm and intrigue to some of the places we passed through: how and why was a little coastal village called New-Wes-Valley? There was a story there.

Rocks, water, more rocks and piles of mysterious wood

We also came across piles and piles of sawn wood. They were lying everywhere; not just beside houses where we would expect them to be, but along the seashore, piled on rocks, or along the side of the road, sometimes in a field and sometimes in amongst the many piles of rocks. We wondered what this wood was for. Near a house we could imagine it was for heating, and perhaps by the shore the wood would be used for smoking fish. But out in the fields, or amongst the rocks in the middle of nowhere? It was a really strange world, especially as some of the stacks looked as if they had been there for years, while others looked new. We were left puzzling over this, and never did learn quite why they were there.

We finally arrived at Terra Nova Provincial Park in the late afternoon, and settled in for the night. We still had some of the fresh frozen cod we had bought in Twillingate, so we thought this was the appropriate time for fish chowder. It was a very satisfactory end to an interesting day, and the fresh frozen fish was so much better than any we can buy at our local supermarket. We didn't see much of Terra Nova itself, as this was just a quick stop for the night. In retrospect, perhaps lingering a little would have shown us yet another aspect of Newfoundland's natural beauty.

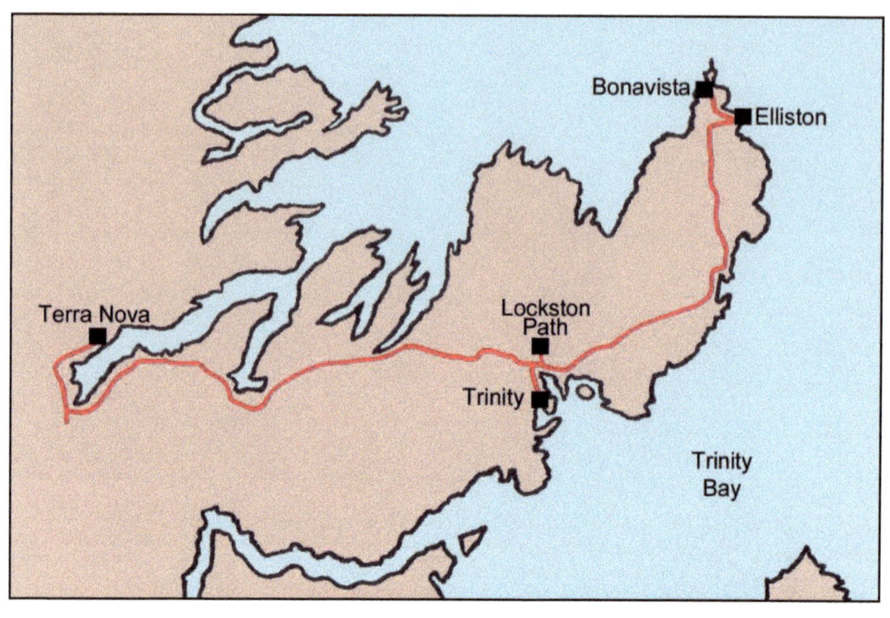

Terra Nova to Lockston Path	138km
Trinity to Bonavista	89km
TOTAL	227km

Chapter Eleven

Terra Nova to Bonavista

Years ago, Bob had visited the picturesque town of Trinity in his professional capacity with the Canadian Conservation Institute, and was anxious to show me the charms of this little place. So we left Terra Nova early in the morning and headed in that direction. We paused for a few moments in Port Blandford, a picturesque little village, for yet another photo op and noticed yet another huge pile of logs rotting away. We arrived in Trinity in mid-morning and immediately fell in love with its picturesque qualities.

One of many views of this picturesque place that features in so many descriptions of the 'typical' Newfoundland

Our first stop was the museum that Bob visited so many years ago. As we walked by the displays in this lovely little building, Bob noticed a sextant incorrectly labelled as a quadrant. He smiled; this was an 'old friend', as he had mentioned this small error on his previous visit. Like the staff in so many of these small places, they were primarily volunteers and so the labeling had never been changed. After a thorough examination of the collections, we asked the staff where to find a good place for lunch. The first place recommended was the Dockside Café, a really nice looking restaurant, but it was completely full and had a long wait time, so we consoled ourselves by visiting the *chocolatier* and tasting their offerings. Naturally, this led to buying some of their wonderful produce. (Note to self: never enter a *chocolatier* when you're hungry.) Finally we made our way to the Mercantile Café, the second recommended spot. Bob enjoyed his seafood chowder, while I was happily satisfied with a very tasty, large and freshly-made sandwich. We shared the delicious partridgeberry dessert before continuing our explorations.

Trinity lies on a peaceful bay in a sheltered arm of the sea

Once at the Visitors Centre we learned about the Rising Tide Dinner Theatre, and so after our positive experience in Twillingate we decided to see what the show was all about. At the box office we had a reality check! The Twillingate Dinner Theatre had been quite a casual affair, but with the fame of this one we ran the serious risk of a sold-out show. Thankfully, the ladies in the box office squeezed us in as extra guests, but being late-comers we had the meal choice of roast beef or roast beef! So we chose the roast beef.

With our evening plans now settled we visited the historic houses open to the public, and learned some of the history of families living here. Who knew that Trinity was the first place in North America where smallpox vaccination was practiced? There was a wonderful display in one of the houses describing the story of the Rev Clinch—a medical doctor before his ordination as a minister—who was a colleague and childhood friend of Dr Edward Jenner. Through him he learned the benefits of vaccination, so here in Trinity he treated his own children and eventually many of the townspeople. This first known use of smallpox vaccination in North America occurred around 1800, and the benefits of it were seen shortly after when a ship carrying the disease docked in the harbour. Individuals in the local population were able to nurse the sick in the knowledge they would be immune from this frightening disease. Rev Clinch shared this information with Jenner, who made sure that the Reverent continued to receive supplies, and had this effective vaccine always on hand.

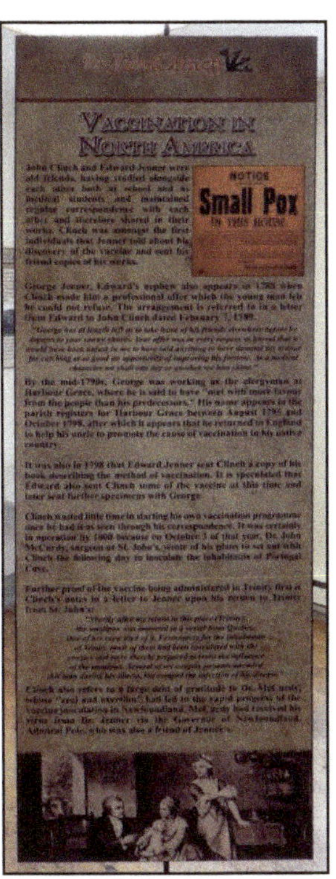

Our next stop was the forge, and here we spent quite a bit of time. We were interested to learn that the leather and wood bellows used for heating the coals dated from the late 19th century and, apart from a few patches, were still in great shape and used every day. We watched the blacksmith at his craft, and were impressed with the fine work he was doing. His wrought ironwork was for sale, and there were some really interesting items, including a beautiful coat rack. He told us he shipped orders across Canada, so he might well be hearing from us.

(Left) The forge bellows still working after a century of use

(Below) The blacksmith tending his hearth

After this very useful visit we dropped into the cooperage and had a very interesting chat with the docent there. He demonstrated the use of a bow drill and naturally Bob tried it. After a couple of false starts he succeeded in drilling a small hole with this old technology. It really wasn't as easy as it looked, but no doubt had he more time he would have become quite proficient.

Our final port of call was the Anglican Church. This large building has some lovely woodwork throughout and, as Bob discovered, the organ was very similar to the one in Twillingate, and of the same vintage. As with all churches, we enjoyed examining the stained glass windows, and we both really appreciated the one dedicated to all the craftsmen who had been involved in the building of the church (see p. 173).

The Trinity Anglican church

It had been a very busy day, and our dinner theatre appointment was looming, so prior to our evening's entertainment, we moved the RV from its place near the museum to a much larger parking area closer to the Rising Tide building, just so it would be easier to leave later in the day. We found this dinner theatre to be a more formal experience than the Twillingate theatre. We were greeted with a printed program, which included bios of the performers, and discovered that the Rising Tide Theatre was a professional company. We were seated at long tables with benches, which seems to the pattern for this kind of entertainment. While we waited for dinner we chatted with the couple opposite us who had also been squeezed into the dinner at the last minute. They too were having the roast beef! Our neighbours described the walking pageant presented by The Rising Theatre Company, where the performers act out the history of the area in various locations throughout the town where the action would have taken place. We had seen some of these skits in passing as we explored the town, but had not realized how extensive the tour was, and how much history it covered. Our fellow guests had completed the walk and found it really informative and enjoyable.

After a very good meal, the show started. This performance was more polished and professional than the one in Twillingate, but much less inclusive. We missed the interaction between the players and audience that we had so enjoyed previously. The program consisted of a variety of well-known songs and music from the locale, interspersed with monologues and a very amusing play in which Dracula visited Trinity. The evening finished with more songs, but even though most of audience probably knew them, they seemed less inclined to join in. Nevertheless, we really enjoyed this evening and thought it an appropriate closing to our visit to Trinity.

It was late by the time we left Trinity and located our chosen campsite, Lockston Path Campground, several kilometres away. Access entailed a long stretch on a gravel road, but fortunately the campground was a very attractive and a lovely place to stay for the night, which more than made up for our driving *déjà vu*. It was such a charming and restful spot that we would have been happy to stay there an extra night, but Bonavista was calling our names.

This leg of the journey was marked by detours from our planned route because, heading directly to Bonavista, we were drawn towards Elliston. Our only excuse was the description in the guidebook, 'Elliston, the Root Cellar Capital of the World'. With a description like this, who could miss visiting? So, naturally, we found ourselves in Elliston—accessed by a rough but passable road—examining several of the famed root cellars. After all, this little place has over 140 of them, dotted all about the landscape and just looking cute!

Before refrigeration these root cellars were used for the storage of vegetables and other perishables. In the summer, milk, cream, cheese and any other items that required cooling were stored next to the vegetables. These low buildings are basically sod houses, either dug into the existing landscape or built on the surface, perhaps behind a house or some other convenient location. As we peeped inside a couple of them we noticed they had been partitioned, perhaps because they were used by more than one family. There was the shelving all-round the walls, which increased the storage space of these useful little buildings.

A peep into one of the root cellars open to the public

Year-round, the internal temperature would be generally cool but not freezing, rather like a modern day refrigerator, so it would not be really suitable for the long-term storage of meat or fish. Looking at the inside of them reminded me of the ice house dug into the permafrost that we had seen in Tuktoyatuk, where hunters and their families stored food in order to preserve it. It was a great way to employ the natural environment. Here in Elliston and many other places in the east, root cellars were used for many years as the only realistic way of preserving perishable items before the availability of modern cooling methods, so when electricity and fridges became more common the use of the cellars decreased. Interestingly, according to a couple of local people, even though they had the convenience of a fridge in the home, some of the older generation kept to their ways and have stuck to their root cellars for food preservation.

Why the Root Cellar Capital of the World? Here is the economic and creative genius of the Elliston townsfolk: with the collapse of the cod fishing industry in the 1990s Elliston was facing severe economic hardship, so to encourage tourists to this isolated spot, they realized this unique resource and very cleverly advertised the place, firstly as the

Root Cellar Capital of Newfoundland. It was only later they discovered that nowhere else in the world has as many root cellars as this little place!

We were fortunate that the root cellars had drawn us to Elliston because an even greater drawing card for tourism is the huge and very accessible puffin breeding spot. This is a must-see for birdwatchers of the world, and a joy for the casual observer. Every year thousands of puffins arrive in May to breed on the rocky outcrops, then leave in mid-August after the single chick each breeding pair produces has fledged. We walked out along a narrow path to the colony at the tip of a headland. Fortunately, the breeding area is on a large rock separated from the headland by a rather nasty, rocky and deep cleft, which means it is impossible to actually access the breeding area. The gap is too large to jump, yet close enough to allow the visitor excellent viewing conditions.

Puffins and gulls sharing the habitat

Puffins are funny little birds, and to see them in such masses was a treat. There were also many gulls, but all the birds seemed to get along quite well. We watched the puffins as they went about their parental duties, waddling comically and then flying gracefully to find food for themselves and their single chick. It was such a joy to see these pretty birds, and a wonderful surprise since we had not known the colony existed before arriving in Elliston.

The puffins' nests are small holes in the ground where the chick resides until fledgling

Before leaving Elliston we paused for refreshments at the local restaurant. It is housed in a very attractive building converted from the local Orange Lodge. The owner told us all about the upswing in the village's economy since the 1990s, and it was clear that the villagers themselves had created the increase in tourism, and hadn't waited for the government to step in. It was an uplifting story of the successful recreation of an economy, and one that I feel should be more widely known.

Enough of the detours!—although, when they are like Elliston they are wonderful and not to be missed—but Bonavista was still waiting. We were continuing our 'lighthouse tour', so naturally our first stop was the Bonavista lighthouse. Fortunately the weather remained clear and warm with not a fog bank in sight; very different from our last lighthouse experience in Twillingate. We first explored the little museum in the lighthouse keeper's family residence. Occasionally two families would be expected to share the residence, which might have been a challenge, or perhaps because of the isolation, a much happier situation. After perusing the exhibits we climbed to the lighthouse itself. This is a funny little building, quite short and stubby. Because of its high elevation on a rocky promontory, the light-keeper had only 20 steps to climb before he was at the level of the light itself. This was a change from the previous lighthouses we had visited, where there were many flights of stairs for the poor keeper to tread up and down each day.

The silvered copper parabolic mirrors that focused the light into a beam were a masterpiece of craftsmanship, as they had probably been formed by hand and burnished to a fine finish and accuracy

The mechanism that rotated the light was fascinating; the weight-driven drive mechanism incorporated a verge escapement to control the rate, an idea superseded in clocks by the pendulum in the 17th century. Basically, there are two little spinning vanes driven by the clockwork, and their speed of rotation is naturally limited by air resistance; they achieve a certain speed, and stay at it. The light-keeper had to wind the mechanism up every two hours during the night, so perhaps he was more fortunate than the keeper of Point Amour, since he only had a few stairs to climb.

The weight-driven drive mechanism with verge escapement in the horizontal wheel on the right

This light, like so many others, has been replaced by a more modern version, and the two lights now sit side-by-side on the headland. The newer light is automated and needs little if any tending. It just does its thing without all the fuss and palaver of the first light, so the romanticism and the old stories of the original lighthouse and its keeper are now just sidelines.

The new light, atop its latticed tower, makes quite a contrast with its solid, old-fashioned predecessor

After leaving the lighthouse we walked to the edge of the rocky shoreline, and looked down on the jagged rocks and surging waves. From this vantage point we could well understand the need to warn ships about these quite beautiful, yet very ugly rocks. Just thinking what damage could be inflicted on a ship was not a pleasant thought. However, on this lovely sunny day the coastline looked beautiful, although on a stormy and cold night it would be a different story.

There have been times when taking our grandchildren for walks that we glibly tell them of the power of the sea, or a river or any other body of water. Now, we had a chance to see just what the sea could really do.

Over thousands of years along this very rocky coastline, caves have been carved out of the rock by the sea. It was here we could really appreciate what the sea can do when given enough time. Not far from the Bonavista light were two huge sea caves side by side; over many years wave erosion united them into one massive cave, which then collapsed in on itself. We didn't know how long ago this had happened, but peering over the edge at the remains of this collapse we could only wonder at the forces at work that caused it. As we walked around this huge cavity, with the sea rushing in and out, we noticed areas of erosion around the top edge, which are no doubt getting bigger year by year. Just for all those who like statistics, we later read that this huge hole is 250 metres in diameter, with a depth of 15 metres. Apparently, some intrepid climbers and cavers have descended to the floor of the cave, not something we plan on doing any time soon! As we scanned the coastline we could see other areas that might have been caves long ago, but are now just semicircular bays of rock, jutting out to sea.

The collapsed sea cave, with its almost sinister expression

After seeing these effects of the forces of nature, and feeling quite small in comparison, we found our way back into the town of Bonavista. High on our list of priorities was a visit to the recreated *Matthew*, the ship that brought John Cabot to Newfoundland. Other sites to see according to our guidebooks included the Mockbeggar Plantation, and The Ryan Premises Historic Site.

We were fascinated by the unusual name of the Mockbeggar Plantation. The origin of the word is unclear, but it was thought to have come from the south east of England. The first settlers may have come from that region, and there is a town in Kent called Mockbeggar. Or perhaps it was from the old word for a building that appears wealthy but is actually derelict? The Mockbeggar Plantation property is thought to be the oldest identifiable fishery in Newfoundland. The long wooden salt-box storehouse is thought to have been built around 1733, and has therefore been in existence for nearly 300 years. During its long lifetime this building has served many functions, including salt fish store, salmon packing house, fish dryer, barter shop, residence, temporary church, headquarters for the Salvation Army, and miscellaneous warehousing in more recent years. Quite the resumé for a rather unassuming building.

The residence on the property was originally built in the 1870s and has undergone many changes since then. In the 1980s the owners of the house donated it to the province, and it was restored to early 20th century period in honour of F. Gordon Bradley, a politician who was influential in bringing Newfoundland into Confederation. The house itself was beautifully appointed, and a pleasure to walk through. One of the rooms (left) was very special to Mr Bradley, and here he kept his books and instruments. It was an unusual room, with its stained glass windows appearing almost like a private church. It would have been so interesting to hear Mr Bradley's views on this room; I am sure he would have had a lot to say.

We then went to find the Matthew Legacy Site, the home of the *Matthew*, a copy of the ship that John Cabot (Giovanni Caboto) sailed across the North Atlantic under the auspices of the English Crown, and 'discovered' Newfoundland. The museum, adjacent to the *Matthew's* dry-dock, tells the story of that voyage through the eyes a member of his crew: the surgeon's apprentice, who later became a ship's surgeon. I really enjoyed this method of telling the story, as it made it really interesting and captured some of the flavour of the actual voyage. The ship itself was a huge surprise; the reproduction shows how small this ship really was. Standing in the middle of the ship and imagining sailing the North Atlantic with a crew of 20, having only sails as a means of propulsion, was mindboggling to say the least. There are RV trailers these days that are almost the length of this ship! It was also very humbling to think of men who would travel the distances they did, in often difficult conditions, in such a craft.

The Matthew is closely enclosed in its dry-dock, appearing even smaller than it really is

From the historical record, it appears Cabot was aware he was heading towards land; knowledge gained probably from the Norsemen who had sailed this way before, but even with all that knowledge, what an accomplishment, and what bravery to head into the almost unknown. When making this voyage he noted the abundance of cod in the seas around Newfoundland and created, though probably with-out realizing it, the east coast fishing industry.

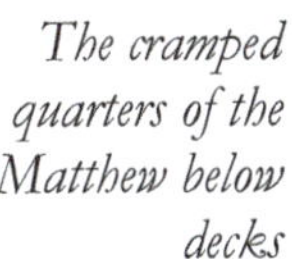

The cramped quarters of the Matthew below decks

Our final exploration for the day was the Ryan Premises National Historic Site. This site exhibits the rich history of the Newfoundland cod fishery and tells the story of the Ryan family who pioneered generations of business success in the fishery.

Several of the Ryan Complex buildings, the wooden construction being very typical of the area

We did see part of this extensive site, and looked at many of the artifacts on display, but by now I have to confess that our hearts, heads and legs were all too tired, so weren't able to give it the attention it deserved. So, after a brief look around, we regretfully left these interesting buildings and found ourselves a campsite for the night, Paradise Trailer Park, just south of Bonavista.

It was time to stop and reflect on all we had seen and learned—and perhaps shuck off our museum and cod fishery fatigue—before traveling on to new and different sites. But in keeping with the day's theme, we enjoyed our pan-fried cod for supper, the last of the fish from Twillingate.

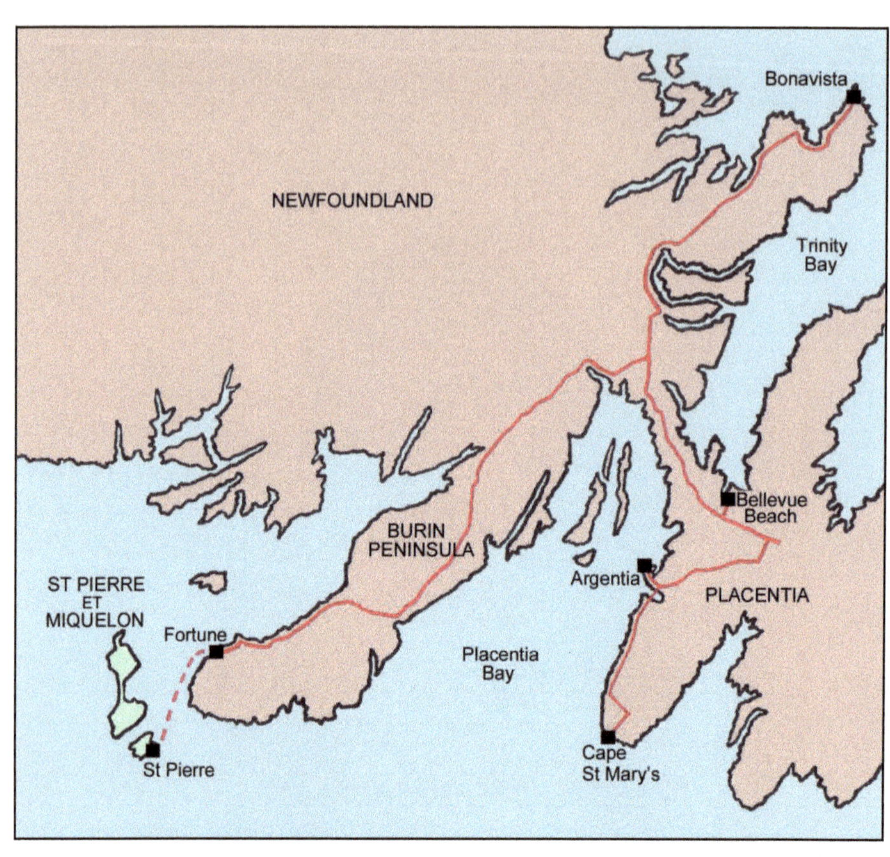

Bonavista to Fortune	346km
Travel within Fortune and environs	13km
Fortune to Bellevue Beach	255km
Bellevue Beach to Argentia	219km
TOTAL	833km

Chapter Twelve
Bonavista to Argentia

When planning this trip, we had tentatively thought that a visit to St Pierre and Miquelon would be interesting, even though we had no idea how feasible a visit to 'France' would actually be. We left Bonavista and drove hopefully south towards Fortune on the Burin Peninsula, the departure point of the ferry to St Pierre. Madame GPS advised us that the drive would take about five hours, so we left the Bonavista area in the morning, planning to arrive in Fortune by mid-afternoon. The drive was quite pleasant, especially the latter part that took us over the Burin Peninsula, through wild and deserted moorland. On this stretch we found ourselves a lovely spot to stop for lunch; a small unpaved road off the highway, which appeared to pass a small stream. We drove down beside the stream and, even though the highway was quite close, we had found a very peaceful place to have lunch while relaxing and watching the water gently flow.

A pleasant stopping spot for lunch

Once in Fortune we inquired at the Information Centre about next day's ferry, and also about a place to stay for that night. The latter was the easy part since Horsebrook Trailer Park is the only one in the area! The ferry to St Pierre was a different story. The ferry schedule was such that we would need to spend the night over on the island, since St Pierre was its home port and it docked there overnight, with the return trip at noon the next day. Only on a Wednesday could you go early in the morning and return in the evening, which was not really helpful as we were there over the weekend. However, we had got this far, and just like our impulsive visit to Battle Harbour, we jumped at the opportunity to spend a night in France. All we had to do was buy the tickets and find somewhere to stay on the island. The Information Centre staff very kindly called the ticket agent, who agreed to meet us the next morning to see if this mini-trip could be arranged. So with all this in place we went to our campground.

As we booked in at Horsebrook we had a lovely conversation with the owner and described our potential visit to St Pierre. This very helpful gentleman told us that the RV could stay where it was, and he gave us a contact for the local taxi service, which would take us from the campsite to the ferry and also meet us on our return. All this for the princely sum of $5.00 each! Now all we had to do was wait and see if the ticket office people could come through with both tickets and a place to say.

The day was done and it was almost time for supper. Out came the Newfoundland muffin and bread book I had bought, what felt like so long ago at the Information Centre in Gros Morne, and I made cheese muffins to complement our supper. They really turned out well, and will be a good addition to my personal recipe book. It was a fitting end to the day.

The morning dawned bright and clear, and we hoped our plans would come to fruition when we arrived at the Ferry Terminal office. The ferry was scheduled to leave at 2:00pm so there was enough time, we hoped, for the staff in the Terminal Office to do their magic and find us somewhere to sleep in St Pierre. The ticket agent told us he was working on finding us a bed-and-breakfast but he needed more time, so he advised us to come back in an hour and hopefully he would have an answer for us. While we were waiting we visited the local arena where the people of Fortune would be hosting an International Lunch. It was only 10:30 or so, but at least we could see what was on the menu. Having satisfied our curiosity we returned to the Ferry Office where we happily heard that the agent had performed a miracle and found us a bed for the night. After confirming the accommodation and buying our ferry tickets, we were all set for our trip to St Pierre.

We still had a couple of hours before the ferry, so it was time to explore the joys of Fortune. Our first stop was the International Lunch, Newfoundland style: Irish stew, Jamaican patties, humus and pita, mulligatawny soup, Mexican eggs, croissants, beans, and Belgian waffles with cream. Quite an eclectic mix of foods and all quite delicious. Of course, we started chatting to people and learning more about the area. After the meal we wandered around the little stalls selling small craft items. Much to my delight, I found a couple of hand towels for the kitchen with crocheted loops, which means they will hang neatly on my oven door. When we finally returned to Ottawa, I took great satisfaction in replacing the previous old and worn out ones with this attractive new addition.

Fortune is famous for its ecological park. It is an extremely important zone in the fossil record where specimens from the so-called Cambrian explosion can be found. Bob has long been fascinated with fossils, so he wanted to explore the area and perhaps find some fossils to add to his collection.

The park is a little way out of town along a well-used gravel road, which ends at a small lighthouse. This attractive building looked quite charming with the sun glinting off the waves in the background, but it was not what we were actually looking for this time. There were no signs indicating the fossil beds, so when we found a small path heading towards the cliff tops we followed it, hoping to find something of interest. The path ended at a rock face and Bob was able to descend the last little part to the rocks below, but before he did this I asked him for the keys. If he fell down the cliffs and into the sea I would still be able to get into the van! The good news was he didn't fall, but the bad news was he didn't find any fossils. We were glad we had a chance to explore this very attractive area, but we wondered about the location of the fossils. We learned later that the fossil beds are difficult and somewhat dangerous to get to, so was not surprising we couldn't find them. In retrospect, it was probably for the best for protection of this national heritage. Now, it was time to go back to our vehicle and prepared it and us for our mini holiday in France.

Our taxi was a small van driven by a very friendly man who has a little business taking people to the ferry and picking them up on their return. How he makes a living at a grand total of $5.00 per person is a mystery. More than reasonable we thought! Naturally, we arrived at the ferry dock far too early and had to wait for its return from St Pierre. We joined the small crowd of passengers and spent some time people watching.

While waiting, Bob got chatting to a guy with a bicycle and dog trailer. He was German and had been traveling with his dog through the Netherlands, Belgium, France, Spain and Portugal. He had then flown the whole outfit to Toronto and had pedaled his way to Fortune from there. As a computer programmer he had set-up his 'office' on the front pannier of his bike, and was able to work from anywhere in the world. All his electronics were powered by solar cells attached to the roof of his dog's trailer, so providing that the weather co-operated he was all set to go. Quite the character.

At last the ferry pulled into the dock and much to our surprise it was a large catamaran. We needed to wait while the passengers disembarked and went through Canadian Customs and Immigration, which served as a reminder that this ferry ride was international. Intellectually we knew this, but we now saw it in practical terms.

The catamaran Le Cabestan *of the Conseil Territorial de St Pierre et Miquelon*

Once the disembarking passengers were through the formalities we were invited on board. At the top of the gangplank were met by an exotic welcoming committee of traditionally-dressed sailors, who waved us aboard. We found some seats next to the window, which needed cleaning, and settled down. After everyone was on board the boat left the dock. For the first 30 minutes or so the sea was quite gentle since we were running parallel to the coast, and were still sheltered by the land. As we turned further out the waves picked up, not hugely but large enough for the catamaran to roll and corkscrew a little. We found this motion exhilarating, but one lady we noticed was looking very green indeed. The motion explained a lot about the dirty windows; on the opposite side of the vessel the windows were continually hit by waves and the water was streaming off them, so the grubbiness was nothing more than dried, crusted salt.

After about an hour of sailing we approached St Pierre and the seas calmed. Even from the sea, we noticed immediately the difference between the buildings of Newfoundland and those of St Pierre, and once on shore it became more noticeable still. While the colours of the houses were as bright and varied, and the roads were not level but rather climbed the hills in the same higgeldy-piggeldy way they do in Newfoundland, there was something different. Certainly, the names of roads and stores were all in French, and the language we heard all around us was French, but there was something else. I really can't explain it: was it the stores, the architecture, the language? Or perhaps a combination of the whole ambience that struck us? We could not decide, but the place felt quite 'foreign'.

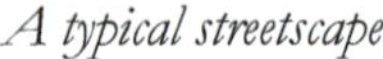

A typical streetscape

Our bed-and-breakfast at the top of the town. The road really was as steep as the picture suggests

After noting where the office of the Comité Régional du Tourisme was located, we walked up a steep road to our bed and breakfast, at the very end where the street stopped at a rock face. We met our voluble French hostess who had lots to tell us, but unfortunately her English was as good as my French (virtually nonexistent) so Bob spent his time listening to her and passing on the information to me. Our room was really comfortable and well furnished; when we looked out of one window we could see the rock face up close and personal, while the other window looked over the very attractive town of St Pierre. After leaving our cases in our room we went back to the Tourism Office to check various events and sites of interest in this little town. Since we had so little time here, we were advised that a bus tour would be a great way to see as much as we could in a short period, and it would also give us some ideas of places we might like to explore on our own. So we bought tickets and while we were waiting we wandered around the town. Luckily, we were in St Pierre for the Basque Festival, part of which was a pelota competition. It was interesting to watch; it looked a bit like squash, played against a wall with a ball and racquet, but instead of a small court, this game was played outdoors in a large area against a huge wall called a fronton. It looked extremely skillful and was great to follow, so we stayed for a while then continued to wander the town.

We had arrived on a Saturday afternoon, which in retrospect was probably not the best of ideas because many of the stores are only open Saturday morning. Unsurprisingly, the liquor store was open, so we went in to see what was on offer. There were a number of rather nice looking wines and scotches, but we left empty handed. It really didn't seem worthwhile for us to bring bottles back into Canada. The fun part of checking out stores is seeing what is actually available, and assessing or guessing the local taste buds.

When it was nearing the time for our bus tour we returned to the Tourism Office. The staff had a unique and useful service to offer: several local restaurants had provided the bureau with their menus. Once we had perusing the offerings and had made our choice, the staff made a booking for us. I could wish other tourist information centres could provide such a service; it was very helpful when exploring unknown territory.

A view of St Pierre harbour during our bus tour

Our bus tour was quite extensive, and we shared the experience with many other tourists who had come over on the ferry with us. The bus traveled all around this small island and our tour guide, a student at McGill in Montreal, knew a great deal about the place and happily shared it with us. The more amusing pieces of information came in the form of statistics. St Pierre and Miquelon have a population of 6,000. There are 5,000 cars to drive around just 25km of road. The roads are narrow with many steep inclines and lots of sharp curves, which in turn result in a multitude of accidents! So much so that the local garage works fulltime just doing repairs! As the bus followed many of these little roads I wondered how people actually managed with so many cars. Most of the roads had cars parked on both sides, and in no particular order. And as pedestrians we felt we were often risking our lives when simply crossing the road! Perhaps this was one of those features that contributed to the European feel of the place?

Steep roads and parked cars made our bus tour quite an experience in careful driving

The roads are a lovely pink colour, which according to our guide is due to the use of the pink volcanic rock that comprises much of the island. Where the rocks were exposed we had seen this predominantly pink colour, so the colour of the roads now made perfect sense. On a small island like this you are never far from the sea, so wherever the bus took us we found ourselves looking out on some wonderful seascapes in every direction. We kept noticing horses in fields and asked our guide about them. These are riding horses, about 300 in total, which stay in the fields for the summer and are stabled during the winter. They added a charming note to the scenery.

The predominantly pink rock of much of St Pierre

At one of our scenic stops we overlooked the strait between the islands of St Pierre, Langlade and Miquelon. The archipelago is somewhat misnamed because the island of Langlade is equally as large as Miquelon yet not mentioned. St Pierre is the smallest of the three. Langlade was directly across from us at our vantage point, while Miquelon was hidden behind it to the north. The two islands are connected to each other by a long sandy causeway, and both are very sparsely populated.

While on the bus tour we talked to the guide about living and working on the island. He described the support the French government provides to students. If they attend university in France there is free tuition, funding for living expenses, and one free flight home every year. If they have chosen to go elsewhere—and many of them attend Quebec schools—the government will again assist with fees, support of living expenses and the provision of funds for one flight home during the academic year. It stuck me how sensible it was to support the youth of St Pierre in their quest for education since, according to our guide, many of them return to the island to live and work.

We passed the jail and were all interested to learn that it only had five cells, but even in such a small place overcrowding becomes an issue; presently there were seven inmates being housed at the government's pleasure. And there appears little chance of anonymity here, as the guide reported: "We know them all." There are 40 police officers posted from France with their families for a term of four years. It is apparently thought of as a choice posting, since the officers tend to regard it as a vacation. Around the corner was the cemetery was a really interesting place to see. And with no crematorium on the island, the graves had to closely packed together. In order to manage it as well as possible, the bones in unknown graves dating back several generations are disinterred and stored in boxes. Anyone with deceased relatives in the cemetery needs to ensure that the graves of family members are acknowledged, otherwise the remains will be removed and stored.

The cemetery from a distance.

We found the bus tour very interesting and worthwhile, and as we had likely driven most of St Pierre's 25 km of roads, it gave us a much clearer idea of what we might want to see the next day.

Our final activity of the day was dinner. Once more, we met several of our tourist acquaintances as they also had reservations at the same restaurant, *Le Feu de Braise*. The food was excellent and very attractively served; Bob thoroughly enjoyed his lobster, while I happily chose duck comfit. We finished with our favourite dessert, crème brulé, which was also excellent; a complete contrast in every way to our fun International Lunch back in Fortune. After coffee it was time to take a short constitutional to help digest the meal, before returning to our accommodation for a good night's sleep.

Breakfast, the next morning was an interesting experience since I don't speak much French and that was the sole language of the table. Fortunately, Bob could chat with our hostess and the other guests, so the general breakfast conversation was a mixture of French and English, which allowed me to follow some of the discussion. It was a simple continental breakfast; pastries and cereal, Nutella and jam on the side, and a naturally bottomless pot of coffee. We had planned to send postcards to the grandchildren from this outpost of France, so we asked our hostess if it was possible to buy some on a Sunday. We were told, because it was Sunday, we would be unlikely to find anywhere open, particularly the post office. We were briefly disappointed until she produced a pile of local postcards and stamps to go with them, so we happily picked out the necessary postcards, and after completing them, posted them later in the day at the post box near the ferry dock.

Now we were free for the morning and could explore this charming but small town. The Tourism Office very conveniently offered courtesy bag storage for tourists, so after dropping our luggage off, we were on our way. Our first port of call was to a coffee shop. After all, if you are in France the coffee shop is the place to be. Even though it was Sunday, we hadn't counted on every single coffee shop being closed. So the next best place was a patisserie, and maybe we would find some nice pastries to bring back with us as well. Well, one place had been opened very briefly it appeared, but by the time we arrived it was closed. So we weren't doing too well in enjoying all things French! Still, not to be daunted by the lack of refreshment, we walked around the town and found it quite fascinating. We noticed the rather attractive Carousel that graced the main square, and greeted us when we arrived. We were happy to see a couple of children enjoying the ride, but did wonder how much use it received.

Walking around we discovered just how hilly the town of St Pierre is. The very small and narrow streets, narrowed even further by all those parked cars, made walking somewhat unnerving. There were few vehicles moving, but these few were being driven very fast, so when it came to crossing the street we took more than the usual care. The first place we visited was the lookout at the top of the town where we found the most wonderful panorama of the area. The elevation gave us a much better perspective of the town and its surroundings, so we could see where we had traveled on the bus tour and how the town sort of perched on the edge of the rock and was gradually climbing up it. We knew our bed-and-breakfast was the last house on the street, and viewing it from this vantage point we could see no way of adding any more houses in that direction. They would have to be built right into the rocky hillside. But no doubt, if they are needed, I am sure the ingenuity of the St Pierre builders and architects would find a way!

From the top of the hill we noticed the church steeple some distance away in the centre of the town, so we slowly meandered down the narrow and colourful streets in that direction. On the way we were amused by the garbage cans. Well, actually, we didn't see the cans themselves; they were nicely enclosed in brightly coloured boxes, some of which were incredibly intricate. Some matched the house to which they belonged (like the one above) in both colour and shape. Others, it seemed, were made purely with decoration in mind. Then, as we walked down one very steep street, we came across a really silly door. It was at street level but barely reached Bob's waist. We wondered what it was for. Were there pixies living on this island? Who knew, but it was fun to speculate.

After our descent of the town we located the church. It was a very attractive place, with some quite beautiful stained glass windows, and was surprisingly large given the size of the town. We guessed that a marriage had been celebrated the previous day, as there were rose petals strewn along the aisle and outside the church. We hoped the happy couple had enjoyed their special day, and that the weather had been good to them. We arrived at the church at around 10:00am and noticed that High Mass was scheduled to start in half an hour. We could see the church was prepared for Mass, so as it came closer to the time we respectfully left the building to the celebrants.

We walked back up the hill to the Basque Festival site, where we watched the preparations for the day. Nothing was ready yet, so after learning that the food concessions would be open at noon we decided to continue our explorations. As we were walking down to the dock area, we started chatting to another tourist couple. They told us that one of the two museums was open, so naturally we headed towards it. We remembered having it pointed out on our bus tour, so it was good to know it was actually open to visitors on a Sunday. The museum building is modern and quite beautiful, although

the display area is quite small. We were directed to an exhibition of photographs of St Pierre and Miquelon, one of which would be chosen by ballot to be reproduced as a postcard for sale in the museum. We thought this was a lovely idea and had great enjoyment choosing the picture we each thought best represented the islands. Bob and I had different ideas, which made it all the more fun. As we moved away from the photograph display we came face to face with the only guillotine in St Pierre. This gruesome artifact had been imported from France many, many years ago for its designated purpose, but thankfully it had only been used once. We decided it was in the best place, since here in the museum it couldn't be used, but would symbolize a very different age.

The exhibits provided a very complete history of St Pierre and Miquelon, particularly the story of cod fishing and its effect, both positive and negative, on the community. This was very similar to the issues faced by Newfoundland with first the wealth and then the sudden collapse of the fishery. (It came home to us how much cod we were encountering, no matter where we stopped on this entire vacation.) We were surprised to discover how many times these small islands had changed hands between the French and the British, appearing to be a small pawn in the game of diplomatic chess. With all the various treaties between the two nations, the citizens went through nine changes of allegiance. Now they are finally French, and the absent but supportive French government assures their viability, with or without the cod.

The museum displays were beautifully laid out and very informative. The modern, custom-designed building gave us a hint as to how much financial support the French government provides to these remote islands

Now it was time for lunch, so we headed back to the Basque Festival. It became clear as soon as we arrived that we were not the only ones focused on lunch! While there was not much cultural activity yet, the food concessions were doing good business. We were directed to buy our tickets from a kiosk set up for the purpose. It was weird to be working in Euros, but as it is the currency of France our minds needed to make the switch. This was the first time we actually needed to pay cash, since we had used plastic for everything else! We chose the concessions where the food looked the most interesting to us; Bob tried cod cooked with peppers and onions, while I had duck confit, and we both had delicious fried potatoes, which tasted as if they had been cooked in the duck fat. Since we were in France, we naturally enjoyed a glass of wine with our meal. The wine was served in plastic glasses (horrors! but probably a sensible idea) but this really didn't spoil our enjoyment of the meal. We finished off with some tasty pastries and felt replete. It was a very good end to an interesting 24 hours in a very different place.

Our cheery servers in their booth decorated with Basque symbols

As we looked around the concessions we saw so many people dressed in the red, green and white of Basque as well as those dressed in the traditional dress of the region. Likely they were part of the celebrations, but it was also a recognition of their history and perhaps their loyalties as well.

People in traditional Basque dress. The red-brown wall, just visible at the right behind the tree, is the fronton where pelota was played

After lunch it was time to head back to the catamaran and to Canada, to continue our exploration of Newfoundland and the rest of the Maritimes. We needed to be in Argentia the following afternoon for the ferry to Nova Scotia, and the start of the next leg of our trip. The ferry ride back to Fortune went quickly since we both dozed for part of the way. When we disembarked we cleared Customs and Immigration, which again felt a little odd. Some of the passengers actually brought items back from St Pierre, which all had to be assessed, and in some cases duty paid. It all felt a little surreal. Our friendly taxi driver was there to meet us, and quickly returned us to the campground and new adventures.

In our travels we had read about Cape St Mary's Ecological Park and the thriving colony of gannets and other birds nesting on appropriately named Bird Rock. We understood from the literature that this was one of the most accessible seabird colonies in North America, so we definitely wanted to add this to our bird-watching resumé. To put this plan in place, we needed to leave Fortune and head towards the lower tip of the western Avalon Peninsula, yet still have time to return and catch the ferry. This meant leaving Fortune right then and there, heading north up the Burin Peninsula and then turning south to Placentia for the bird colony at the southernmost tip, then returning to the ferry terminal at Argentia. The timing was tight, but we knew we could do it. Just to make sure we had somewhere to camp that night, we made a booking at a place about halfway to our destination with the intriguing name of Puttin Paddle.

We left Fortune, still mulling over our brief stay in France, and recalling all we had seen. As we drove north we decided to pop briefly into Grand Bank to check out the lighthouse and streetscape. Bob had taught a conservation workshop at the local museum many years before, but found that much had changed. The museum had been moved to a grand new building, designed very effectively to look like sails, but unfortunately with our travel constraints we couldn't afford the time to visit. We contented ourselves with the lighthouse, which was small, but given the history it must have seen over the last 150 years we were pleased to actually see it.

By this time it was mid-afternoon and we were anxious to find our campsite and get settled for the night. We were scanning the signs for Puttin Paddle as we drove along the highway, but we saw none! This was a bit concerning, and on finally realizing we must have overshot, it was high time to find somewhere else for the night. We eventually came upon a road sign advertising Bellevue Beach campground, and as we thankfully booked in we mentioned to the owner about missing Puttin Paddle. We learned that that particular place is known as a party campground and is very noisy, so the travel gods must have been watching over us as we had missed whatever signage there may have been! Instead, we had found a delightful place right on the ocean and went to sleep to the sound of gentle waves.

Now it was our final day in Newfoundland, and we were taking the ferry in the afternoon, heading towards Nova Scotia. We left the quiet of Bellevue and headed first towards the Ferry Terminal at Argentia where we confirmed our booking. Since we didn't have a cabin reservation we put our names down on the long list of other hopefuls. So with that little chore done, we drove south to Cape St Mary's Ecological Park to view the gannets at Bird Rock.

It was a foggy day, and the narrow road weaved around the various little inlets, up and down the hills, and through little villages with lots of bush and forest in between. The drive seemed to take forever; no doubt driving in the fog created this feeling as we had no real impression of traveling anywhere. We were just cocooned in a white, enveloping blanket. We finally found the turn-off to Cape St Mary's, a good road and well maintained, but given the lack of visibility in the fog it was still something of a challenge. The road was lined with hydro poles, and it was difficult to see more than two poles ahead as they emerged from the mist. This did not bode well for seeing any birds.

We went inside the Interpretation Centre and rather dispiritedly asked where the birds were and what would be the likelihood of seeing them. The staff reassured us we would see them, even in the fog, so we followed a narrow cliff-top path in the direction of Bird Rock. As we trod the path we noticed a number of sheep just wandering about and doing what sheep do. Apparently they belonged to a local farmer who grazes them there. As we came closer we began to hear a noise that we couldn't identify, and the closer we got to the bird colony, the louder it became. We began to realize this was the sound of hundreds and thousands of birds living and breeding close together on the rocky shore. Finally, we approached a towering pinnacle of rock absolutely covered with gannets, thousands of them, moving all over the rock, nesting and taking off in search for food for themselves and their young. It was almost unbelievable. We just stood and watched them for quite a while, before even thinking about our timing for the ferry. We also identified some of the other birds indigenous to the area, notably murres and kittiwakes, but they were in nowhere near the huge numbers of the gannets. All these birds were in their breeding quarters, so we were able to watch a number of baby birds, just waiting for food, eating and growing. I don't think any of the young birds were fledglings, and we could only imagine what it would be like when they finally took off in the fall. As we made our way back to the Interpretation Centre we were really glad to have made the foggy drive out to see these beautiful creatures. It was well worth the effort and a great finish to our time in the beautiful island of Newfoundland.

The aptly named Bird Rock

The noise of thousands of birds squabbling over the rocky cliffs was matched by their penetrating smell, which we noticed at about the same time we first heard them

It was astonishing to be so close to these beautiful birds in their natural habitat

We drove back to the ferry terminal and finally boarded the ship. We weren't able to upgrade to a cabin, but I did manage to snag blankets from the purser's office for use during the night. As we explored the vessel we came upon the lovely dining area, and in short order we decided to enjoy a luxury meal while traveling to Nova Scotia. It was really enjoyable, and made up for the lack of a cabin.

We settled in one of the lounges and chatted with a couple of people. We recognized one of the bikers we had seen in the line-up prior to boarding. He told us about his roaming lifestyle, describing his winters spent in Mexico and his summers in Canada, and lots of traveling in between. He and his wife had been biking around Newfoundland and tent camping, which with the mostly rainy weather had not proved to be the best experience. His wife was looking forward to the warmer weather of Mexico, which certainly resonated with me. Later on that evening we wandered into the lounge area of the ship and started a conversation with a couple sitting there. They were from Scotland, had rented a car in Halifax and had spent three weeks traveling around the Maritimes. We both exchanged stories about the places we had been, and we showed them some of our pictures of Newfoundland and Labrador, while they shared their experiences of the other Maritime Provinces. This was their third trip to Canada, and they were continually fascinated by the size and diversity of the country. Each time they are here they spend time exploring a different area. No doubt they will be back again at some point.

It was now getting late, and we watched with a degree of envy as they left for their cabin! We tried sleeping in the large and more comfortable airline type chairs, but with little success. In the end I went back down to the lounge, and although there was some light in the room, with the help of the blanket I had been given I was able to lie flat on a couch and sleep for several hours. At one point I woke up and found Bob had joined me and was sleeping on another couch. It was not the best solution, but at least we had some sleep and woke somewhat refreshed at a reasonable hour in the morning.

After our 'interesting' night, Bob and I had the buffet breakfast. It was very much upscale from the breakfasts available on the ship to Nain, but then it also cost more! As we sat over our breakfast we were reflecting on the four weeks we had spent driving through Newfoundland and Labrador, and we both thought it would be great to come back in the future and see some of the many places we had missed. This was a beautiful province to visit, with so many places to explore, so maybe in a few years we will be back. In the meantime, Nova Scotia awaited.

Goodbye to Newfoundland. Until next time…

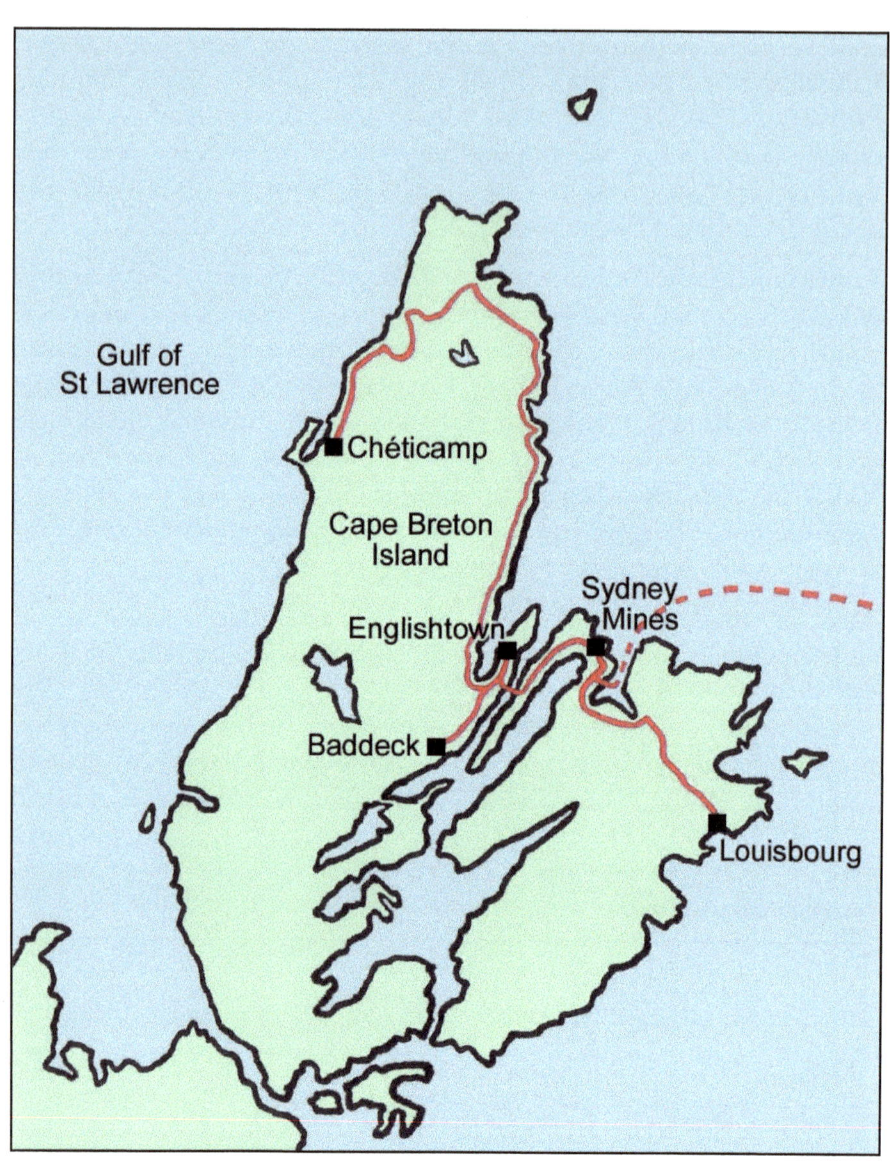

North Sydney ferry to Little Bras d'Or	12km
Little Bras d'Or to Englishtown	270km
Englishtown to Chéticamp	188km
TOTAL	470km

Chapter Thirteen
North Sydney to Chéticamp

We finished our breakfast as the ferry approached the dock at North Sydney. Our first view of Nova Scotia was of a long coastline, and very populous by Newfoundland standards. We drove off the ferry wondering where we would start our explorations. Our only clear plan at this stage was to drive around the Cabot Trail and then turn south for a visit to friends living in Windsor, with a few places of interest interspersed.

Our first glimpse of Nova Scotia

Minutes after we began to drive I noticed a sign advertising a fossil museum, so this seemed an obvious place to start. Since Bob had been unable to even find the fossil beds in Fortune, I hoped this would be a better experience. After following some confusing directions we located the Sydney Mines Heritage Museum and Fossil Centre and, much to our surprise, we were able to sign up for a walk to a fossil bed starting in about 15 minutes. When we asked about the likelihood of finding fossils, the staff guaranteed this would happen.

Before leaving the museum the group, about eight of us ranging in age from young children to seniors, listened to the introductory talk by the museum's palaeontologist on the fossil beds in the region and the type of fossils to be found. The exposed rocks are from the Carboniferous period, approximately 350 to 300 million years ago, so most of the fossils are of vegetation such as ferns and trees. After the introduction it was off to the beach at Point Aconi to find and collect fossils. The palaeontologist very kindly offered to drive us there as he was concerned that our RV would have some difficulty with the roads. We were not concerned ourselves, given the rigorous testing the poor machine had survived earlier on, but we certainly appreciated a ride. We parked on a gravel road and were led down a low cliff to the shore, and then hiked along it until we came to the fossil beds. The hike was quite something; rocks, mud and seaweed, which meant slipping and sliding and coping with all kinds of garbage tipped over the low cliffs or thrown down onto the beach. It was not the most pleasant of walks, and it became quite cool as the wind came off the sea. However, when we finally arrived at the fossil beds it was all worth it. Fossils were everywhere. Virtually every rock had some kind of fossil in it; whether it was a leaf or perhaps a fern or even a section of tree bark. Among the larger rocks with fossilized tree bark, I found a seed case! Bob went all over the site looking for bigger and bigger fossils, eventually finding a large but fragile piece of rock-hard clay. It looked like the forest floor in fossil form, and showed the variety of plants that had lived over 300 million years ago. This precious piece was carefully packed and padded for its successful trip to Ottawa. Bob has plans for displaying it at some point, but still needs to work out how to prevent it from crumbling. This is still a work in progress, and soon we hope to have this wonderful piece on show. The whole group was fascinated by the fossils and we were there for quite some time, searching and locating a variety of flora.

As we were searching—or in my case sitting on a low and comfortable rock—we watched the rain come in, which made the footing for the return trek all the more treacherous. So by the time we made it back to the car we were somewhat wet and muddy to the knees, which necessitated a quick change once we got back to our RV parked at the museum. Clean and dry once again we explored the museum displays. Among the very impressive displays were huge fossil trees that had been found in these strata, often during coal mining operations. While at the beach we had seen these narrow bands of coal running through the crumbling strata, along with pockets of sulphur-bearing rock.

Leaves and tree bark exposed after more than 300 million years

This little excursion was one of those totally spontaneous and wonderful experiences that seem to characterize our travels. We had no idea when we came off the ferry that such and interesting experience was waiting for us, and it encapsulated our views of travel and exploration. We enjoy visiting places we didn't know existed, and we frequently find that these experiences seem to resonate most deeply with us.

There are also places we plan to visit, of course, and now we were here in Nova Scotia the first of those was Louisbourg. This would be our destination on the following day. We drove to the evocatively-named Arm of Gold Campground in Little Bras d'Or, and spent an afternoon dealing with all the domestic chores that had accumulated.

The morning found us in Louisbourg, a drive that brought home to us once again a difference in scale we often perceived between regions. Being used to driving long distances between destinations in Ontario, a quick glance at the map indicated a longish journey to Louisbourg. But there's a lot packed into a small space in Nova Scotia, so we got places much sooner than anticipated. While it takes some time to get used to the different scale, our GPS regularly and quickly corrects our quick-glance notions of the length of projected journeys.

The approach to the fortress of Louisbourg (left) and a view of the Citadel

Louisbourg was just over an hour from our campsite, and so we soon found ourselves thrust into the life of a large mid-18th century fortress. The original buildings had been destroyed, abandoned or naturally deteriorated since the mid-18th century when the site was last occupied by the French. In the early 20th century serious work was done researching its history, and finally in the 1960s archaeological excavations were begun. This work incurred further research as foundations were soon discovered under the soil. Ultimately, in view of all the excavations and ongoing research, it was decided by Parks Canada to rebuild as much as possible using the plans and records of the period, many of which had been discovered in archives in France. So, while much of the present site is a reconstruction, it is all based on existing foundations and solid historical research. As a result, the reconstruction is as accurate as it can be, given the length of time since its destruction.

As a sidebar to the reconstruction project, at the time it was underway the coal fields of Cape Breton were closing down, so many of the miners were retrained to do this exacting work and to learn new trades in the process, which was a very positive outcome for those who had lost their employment.

The Citadel is a very elegant building, appearing here much as it must have done during its heyday in the 18th century

Parks Canada has set the site up in a very attractive manner. There was ample parking, including spaces for buses and RVs, and on entering the Interpretation Centre we found a fine display of the history of the area. We were anxious to get to the site itself, so we chose to save the display area for our return. In retrospect, we found it more helpful to have seen the fortress first, because it enhanced our understanding of the exhibition about it. Visitors are taken by shuttle bus to the actual site, a good distance around the bay, which insulates it from modern incursions. The bus drives you back in time, or so it appears. Seeing the site from the across the bay, situated on its headland, gave an understanding of the strategic importance of the location.

Once off the bus, a fisherman's hut and a local tavern were the first buildings to be visited. Since time immemorial, transportation of any kind has always stopped close to taverns, hostelries, hotels and so on. So why should Louisbourg be any different? After a cursory examination, we continued in a group to the gate of the fortress where we were accosted by a sentry/gatekeeper carrying a very long musket.

He addressed every visitor entering Louisbourg, just like at any other border crossing: "Identify yourself," "What ship are you from?" "What is your business here?" It is a very effective introduction to the garrison, and set the mood for the rest of the day. Then, to deepen the ambience we came across actors in traditional dress who were acting out various historical scenes. From what we could observe, the skits all appeared amusing and comical, although it is hard to judge since we didn't watch them too closely. We were enjoying just wandering around and seeing as much as we could.

Bob was keen to check out the blacksmith's shop, as he had done in L'Anse aux Meadows, but was quite disappointed at the quality of the offerings. There was a demonstration of iron-working underway where a blacksmith was instructing an apprentice. It was bit surprising to see the apprentice holding the hammer in the middle of the handle instead of gaining maximum leverage at the end, and hammering iron that had long since lost its red glow. The problem was compounded when the blacksmith took over and did exactly the same thing! These two would never have been able to create a tenth part of the ironwork needed for working fortress if they couldn't work the metal hot or even hit it hard enough!

Authenticity wasn't at the top of the agenda in the blacksmith's shop, although the tools and equipment were consistent with 18th century practice

Our disappointment with the blacksmith's shop was soon mitigated by the smells from the bakery. As we went in we quickly realized the baker and apprentices did know what they were doing; making really good bread. What could a poor visitor do, but buy a couple of small loaves for future enjoyment?

One of the most exciting things we came across was the foundations of a couple of the original buildings. While we understood that the recreated structures all around us had been built using original plans, to see these actual foundations laid down so many years ago, and to read the plaques describing the history and ownership of the buildings, was quite wonderful. It says a lot that we found the original vestiges of buildings far more interesting than reconstructed houses, actors in costumes and street theatre.

The original foundations of one of the dwellings

We had a fascinating conversation with one of the interpreters who had lived in the area as a child. Her family home had been expropriated in the 1960s because it occupied a site slated for the restoration. She described playing in the ruins as a child and having no concerns of any danger. The children of the area would occasionally find bones, which they just took for granted. Now, many years later, she is very happily working as an interpreter in her childhood haunts. We were visiting the Garrison Chapel at this point, and she gave us a brief social history of this particular part of the complex. Apparently, the townspeople would attend chapel for morning mass as this was the only religious house in this area. Originally there were plans to have a second church built for the townspeople, but church politics had intervened. Another church would have created a second sphere of religious influence, thus undermining the religious hierarchy of the garrison. Rather than allowing this, the townspeople were all encouraged and welcomed to attend services the Garrison Chapel.

The chapel has been beautifully recreated

Like so many recreated historic sites, there were a number of demonstrations of life of the times. Necessarily, since this was a fortress, there were musket and cannon drills, which were entertaining to watch, although a stark reminder of the reality of the original use for this facility. At lunchtime we headed for the Tavern, which was purported to be set up in the 18th century style. There were long tables with benches either side seating between eight and ten. We were beginning to enjoy this informality, and the resulting conversations with other tourists or travelers we met on our trips. We found places to sit and ordered the pea soup, which was thick and generous. The 'coarse bread' was made on site, and was the typical bread of the working man, or in this case the garrison's soldiers. This was the same kind we had bought earlier, so enjoying some at lunchtime was a bonus.

We were most impressed with Louisbourg, and the huge amount of work done to recreate this incredible place, but we both felt it needed several visits to truly appreciate all it had to offer. So next time we are in the area there's still another place to visit.

Our next planned stop was the Alexander Graham Bell Museum in Baddeck. This was a real contrast to Louisbourg but equally as fascinating. When I think of Alexander Graham Bell I just consider the invention of the telephone. After all, we all know about Ma Bell and many of us pay her on regular basis for our phone/internet/television to this day. I did know that some of the work around the telephone was related to Bell's work with the deaf. What I am ashamed to admit is my lack of knowledge of everything else he did. Aside from his work helping with the deaf population with communication, and his development of the telephone, he built flying machines, hydrofoils, and even an iron lung, although it was not really used in the way he envisaged. As far back as 1914 he wrote papers on the dangers of creating greenhouse gases by the burning of fossil fuels, something which has only now become generally recognized. The museum exhibited numerous other inventions and developments, showing what a polymath this amazing man was. Not a bad CV for one person!

Reproduction of the hydrofoil HD-4

The museum display is set up as a timeline of Bell's life, but this wasn't obvious when I first entered the building. It was only after following the exhibits and display panels—which are so well done—that I realized the way the progression and timeline of his life had been laid out before me. There was so much to see that it is hard to select a specific 'best piece'. Suspended from the ceiling of the main hall was a full-sized replica of the *Silver Dart*, the first aircraft flown in Canada, and underneath this was a replica of the HD-4 hydrofoil designed by Bell. We were able to compare the replica with the remains of the original HD4, which is on display as well. The original shows all the signs of major deterioration after it was beached and abandoned, but even in its damaged condition it is quite impressive to see. Bob had visited this museum before so he knew what to expect, but for me it was a wonderful and very inspiring place to visit.

The HD-4 at speed on the Bras d'Or Lake

Having touched a couple of the main historic icons of Cape Breton, it was time to find the Ridge Camp campsite in Englishtown and prepare for driving the Cabot Trail. We had heard many tales about the Cabot Trail, including some from our oldest son who had been a member of one of the Cabot Trail Relay teams, and had run some of the 17 legs of the race to victory, as well as driving his team's support vehicle. Finally, we would see it for ourselves. During our travels we had also met others who had driven the Trail and had told us all kinds of horror stories. Still we were confident the road couldn't be *that* bad, or could it? We knew we would soon find out.

We understood there was a ferry from Englishtown across St Ann's Bay, and because we enjoy ferry trips we thought it might be feasible to take the camper across. Unfortunately, the regular ferry was undergoing repairs and the loading ramp on the replacement one was too steep for the RV, so we had to head back the way we had come from the highway, and then go around the end of St Ann's Bay to the start of the Cabot Trail.

The road was nowhere near as terrifying as we had been promised by earlier fear-mongers. It was in good condition and the views along its length were spectacular. So much so that we made several stops just to admire and photograph the scenes. A major part of the Cabot Trail is in the Cape Breton Highlands National Park, while the rest is maintained by the local municipalities. This does mean the quality of the road surface varies, but generally speaking it was good. The challenge, of course, is the nature of the terrain, which the road follows intimately. It goes up and down and round and about, and is fascinating to drive. As always with this kind of road, you wonder what the next corner or hill will reveal. We climbed several mountains, with very tight curves, steep grades and restricted speed limits. The speed limits need to be respected; they really do reflect the maximum speeds one should go. But there never was a time when we felt our vehicle was stressed or at risk. It made us wonder about the driving abilities of the fear-mongering group!

Vistas such as this became commonplace

We passed through many little towns filled with craft stores, cabins for rent, hotels and B-and-Bs, and so on, all demonstrating how popular this area is for tourism. We saw lovely little beaches and wonderful vistas of sea, sand, rocks and headlands. It was all quite beautiful and had its own particular charm. Although the highlands of Cape Breton are similar in geology to Newfoundland, there is a definable though subtle difference. The only way I can describe the difference, is that these hills appear softer. This may seem an odd way to talk about them, since they are still very rugged and harsh, it is just the overall impression of mountains with more vegetation and perhaps, who knows, more weathering. Whatever the difference, to have seen and closely compared both terrains was a wonderful gift.

The terrain appears softer than the same geology in Newfoundland

Once inside the National Park we located the Park Information Centre, and booked a campsite for that night at the other side of the park. We also acquired a number of maps, including hiking trails, which we decided to try after studying a couple of them closely. So, armed with all this information, we continued driving this amazing road. Naturally we stopped at a variety of look-offs to *Ooh* and *Aah* at the views, and at one point we descended to the shoreline and walked along the beach for a brief distance. My poor camera was red hot with all the picture taking!

A brief and relaxing walk along the beach

In view of our brief time here, we chose only two walks; a trail to the Mackenzie Falls followed by the Skyline Trail, which had been strongly recommended by the Park staff. After a quick lunch we made our way to Mackenzie Falls. This walk is only about 1.7km, and meanders beside a charming rushing stream. It is a loop, so once we found the very attractive waterfall at its top end, and spent some time admiring it, we returning the other way.

The contrast between the two sides of the loop was really interesting. The first part of the trail had consisted of the usual rocks and roots and an occasional narrow pathway, while the other side was less rocky and took us through the forest. There was a huge variety of fungi; red ones, yellow ones, green ones, brown ones, orange ones, sickly white and so many more. It was enjoyable and quite a challenge trying to capture as many as possible on my camera, and I am sure I missed a few. Bob did not recognize many of them, so at some point we will try to identify those unknown to us. By the time we returned to the vehicle we were laughing about our rather amusing walk.

There were probably more fungi that escaped our notice on this short walk

Our next stop was the Skyline Trail, which was much closer than we had thought. We were once again fooled by the map, and had no idea of the true distances between things! Our clue that we must be coming close was the number of cars in the overflowing parking lot and alongside the road. We managed to find a parking spot on the side of the rather narrow road. This was a bit disconcerting, but since everyone else was doing it we just followed suit!

This walk is one of the most popular on the Cabot Trail and we were curious to find out why. There are two sections of trail: a walk of 3.5km to a look-off at the end, returning the same way, and a loop of around 9.5km starting and finishing at the parking lot. This longer one goes to the look-off and then leads away from it, through other areas of the highlands and finally back to the start. We chose to do just the out-and-back route.

The trail itself was an easy walk with a graveled pathway and occasional sections of boardwalk. It was peaceful as it wound through softwood trees interspersed with masses of ferns. After a while the foliage opened up to a savannah type area, which we learned was the result of spruce bud worm. The spruces had died, and other vegetation had taken over, including beech, thus making the area ideal for the moose that had become a major feature of this changing habitat. There is an ongoing experiment in one area. Part of it has been fenced off to keep out the moose, which will then allow the naturalists to discover which trees will naturally take over from the spruce without interference from the moose. It is a long-term experiment and results won't come for several more years.

The test area with information board inset

As we continued our walk the habitat changed once more, with fewer trees and more ground cover, including blueberries and raspberries. What a wonderful place for bears to enjoy. As we approached the boardwalk that led to the end of the trail the vista opened out. Now we knew why this trail was one of the most popular in the park.

The view from the top and the dizzying way down to the lower viewing platform

The view was amazing, wonderful and any every other adjective you could think of. From the look-off at the top, a ladder of wooden steps interspersed with decks, dizzily descended the cliff to a point of rock perched at the very end. The outlook was awe inspiring, as we looked straight out onto the Gulf of St Lawrence from a great height. To say it was breathtaking is to minimize the experience. We spent some time there, just looking out to sea and scanning along the coast. We thought we had spotted some sea mammals in the water, but while they were too far away to identify, just knowing they were there was joy enough. We were loath to leave this glorious place, so after some time we dragged ourselves away and walked back to our vehicle. On the return journey the weather deteriorated and now we were being rained on. We hurried as fast as we could while recalling the sights we had enjoyed so much. In our view this is one of those 'must see' places, and we could certainly recommend it to anyone traveling through Cape Breton.

The Cabot Trail continued to offer wonderful sights, too numerous to mention but all worth seeing, as we continued our drive along the west coast to the Parks Canada campground at Chéticamp. Once we were settled it was time to check what evening activities might be scheduled. It was here we learned about Gaelic singers and storytellers who would be at the community centre that evening, presenting the history of Gaelic speakers in the area. This was a real draw and proved to be a most interesting evening. The two speakers, a man and a woman, spoke of the history of the displaced Scots who had come to Cape Breton. They had brought and maintained the music of their 18th century home in a relatively pure form. In Scotland, as in so many other places, the music of the people has changed over time and in its present iteration no longer represents the old forms, or at least does so in a diluted and transformed way. However, here in Cape Breton the music has remained pure and is being appreciated as a living example of 18th century practice.

We heard how the songs had been used as a means of timing everyday activities. It could be the timing of oar-strokes, or perhaps maintaining a rhythm when reaping hay, or fulling newly-woven cloth to make it firmer and more usable. Apparently, there is one story told of oarsmen who would sing while they were rowing, but as they came into shore they would stop singing because now they could hear the women singing as they fulled cloth or went about their other tasks. Apocryphal maybe, but a good story, yes! Fulling wool cloth would entail pounding the newly woven cloth with hands, feet of even some kind of club. This action was a little like kneading bread dough, and it would cause the fibres in the wool to matt together, and by that means thicken and strength the fabric.

The singers are at the back, leading the group's singing while everyone kneads the cloth to the Gaelic lyrics written on the board

After the history came the music. A bolt of hand-woven cloth was laid on a table with several chairs placed around it. Audience members were asked to come forward and help with the task of fulling the cloth, and soon the table was full, mostly with children who had no shyness about participating. The rest of us were given the chorus in Gaelic and taught how to pronounce the words and then, once we were all ready, the singer began. It was quite fascinating to watch those at the table pound the cloth rhythmically as the singer told the story and, at the end of each verse, hearing everyone join in the chorus. It gave a good feel for what it might have been like so many years ago.

Several songs later it was time to say goodbye. And that was another surprise. There is no word in Gaelic for goodbye, so instead the presenters sang a closing lullaby, a lovely way of ending the evening. Bob and the male presenter spent some time after the show discussing the way the pibroch is judged today. In recent years the focus has been on the speed and accuracy of playing rather than rhythm, which has created a different emphasis and, according to the presenter, not necessarily for the best. Apparently, Scottish pipers who have been introduced to Cape Breton piping have gained a new understanding of where their music came from and how it has changed. Let's hope the pipers of Cape Breton are able to maintain their style of piping as a living historical record. We were pleased to have learned that Gaelic language and culture are so actively encouraged in Cape Breton.

After that wonderful evening it was time to set our sights on Windsor, the home of the friends we intended to visit. So, as we said goodbye to Cape Breton the following morning, we realized we had found yet another place which needed revisiting!

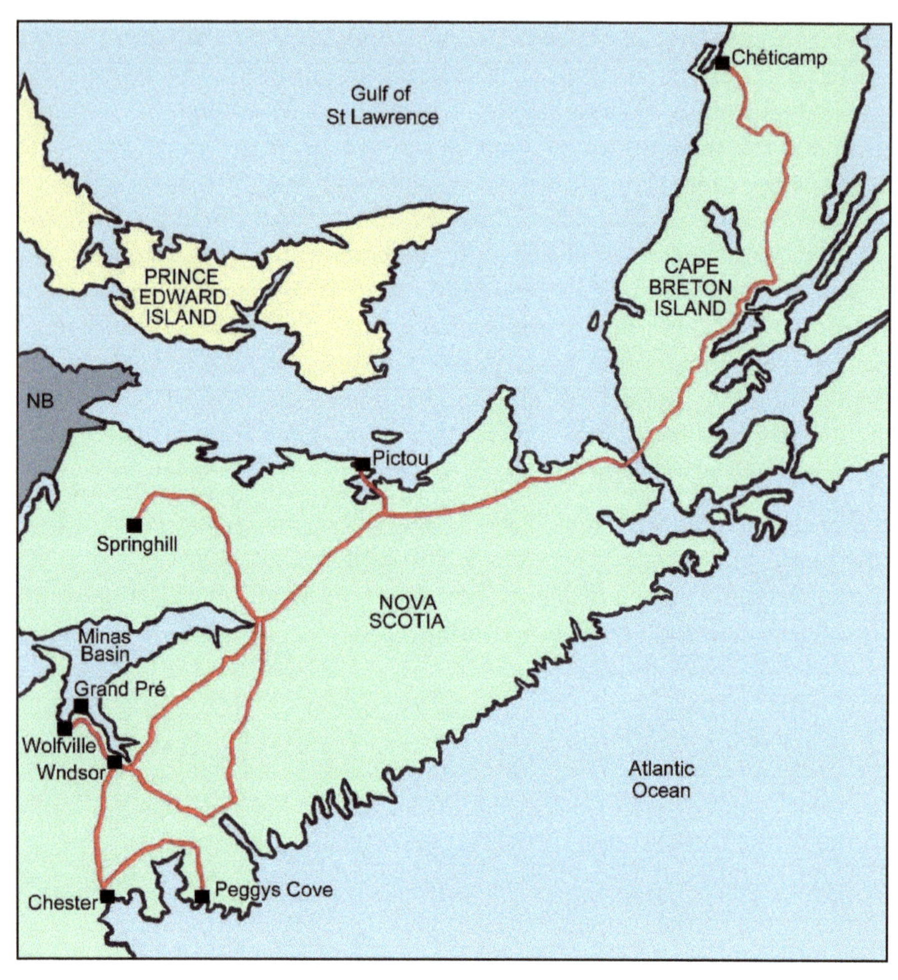

Chéticamp to Windsor	406km
Windsor to Pictou	165km
TOTAL	571km

Chapter Fourteen

Chéticamp to Pictou

After the joys of Cape Breton we headed south to Windsor and our friends, Colleen and Chris. They had moved from Ottawa back to their roots in Nova Scotia, so we were looking forward to catching up with all their news and meeting their extended family. So, when we finally arrived at their home in Windsor after the long drive south, we didn't stop talking until the late evening, there was so much to news to catch up on. We were parked in their driveway so our persistently dripping grey water hose was a bit of an issue, since it really wasn't polite to leak all over their property! Chris and Bob tackled the hose with lots of tools and know-how, and very quickly covered the hole with a stretchy sealant tape, followed by a section of thin sheet metal cut from a Guinness can (two of which had to be emptied first). The hose clamps were reattached and to this day the grey waste water stays inside! I think they did a great job!

Staying with our friends was wonderful. They took delight in showing off their area of Nova Scotia, and were happy to drive us everywhere. Our RV said 'thank you very much' as it sat quietly in their driveway. Our first activity was a visit to the Market Garden in Wolfville, with the command to try the sausages. When we arrived the place was packed, and it seemed that everybody knew everybody else or was related to them. It was such a friendly and welcoming event we immediately felt at home. Bob and I looked around the market, noting the usual veggie, cheese and meat stalls… but wait, it that a beer stall? Yes, and Colleen bought a couple of cans of the locally produced beer. And, oh look over there, I can see some wine merchants. After tasting several of these local offerings (isn't it great to be a passenger?) we came away with a bottle of Tidal Bay white wine. Then we found the 'fast food' section, and I don't mean the Golden Arches. There was so much choice: Indian or Moroccan, sausages or cheese, deli meats and much more, all locally produced. It was all delicious, and some of the sausages found their way into our freezer for future meals.

Now it was on to the local wineries. Way back, when searching through our tourist information we were intrigued to read about the growing wine industry in Nova Scotia, so we suggested a brief wine tour to check out the local produce. Our first stop was at Luckett Vineyards, a lovely location on a small rise, overlooking a valley with the Minas Basin in the distance. Quite beautiful. In the middle of the rows of vines an old-fashioned red telephone box from England could be spied. All guests to the vineyard are invited to call friends and family anywhere in the world, with Luckett's picking up the cost. We were thinking about calling our daughter in England, but unfortunately the line-up was too long! So instead we went inside to try the wines. And what a pleasure that was. We were pleasantly surprised by the quality of their products and after tasting number of excellent vintages we came away with a few bottles.

The view from the Luckett Vineyard. The red telephone box is peeping out among the vines

Next on the winery list was Sainte-Famille, a pretty little place nestled in the countryside a little way south-west of Windsor. Again, we tried a number of the wines and finally settled on one made from Baco Noir, our favourite grape. This was a little different from other Baco Noirs we had tried from the Niagara region, but it was a very nice and pleasant find, and a bottle or two earned the right to be taken home with us!

A lovely reuse for an old church

Our last stop of the day was Avondale Sky Winery. There was quite the story attached to this place. The building is an old church, which was floated on a barge from its original location in Walton on the Minas Basin, then trucked to its present site and set up as a tasting room for the winery. It makes a lovely setting for the wine store and tasting area, and we happily spent a little time tasting before purchasing a couple of bottles to bring back to Ontario.

As contrast to the very attractive, repurposed building, across from the winery was the local church, which is still very much in use today and a reminder of Avondale Sky's origins

It had been a very busy day with our exploration of the market and wineries, so that evening we enjoyed a delightful bottle of Muscat from the Luckett Vineyard and shared our views on life, the universe and everything else.

The next morning our friends took charge, and drove over to the south shore of Nova Scotia. We crossed over the centre of Nova Scotia to our first stop in Chester, a charming little town surrounding a small cove. This is the quintessential vacation spot, with many summer homes, bed and breakfasts, and stores catering to tourists.

Vacation homes in Chester overlooking the harbour

We were in Chester at the end of August, so it didn't seem as busy as it no doubt is in the earlier summer months. Chris knew of a car collector and restorer living in Chester, so we walked over to his house to see some of his vehicles parked at the side of the road. Bob was most taken with a lovingly restored 1946 Willys Jeep, and spent some time admiring it. He also examined several other cars there, but it was clear the Jeep was his favourite.

As always in these little places, we wondered what there was to do, aside from catering to tourism or sailing one of the many boats in the harbour. Then we strolled past the Chester Playhouse Theatre, which is an active element of the community, with a very popular and busy youth program. So this no doubt plays an important part in the community. We were impressed by the number of lovely homes, just the sort you imagine would grace the shores of a fishing village, except for their size. It was amusing to note that they tended to be quite large and frequently had additions in the oddest places, perhaps to include extended family, or maybe to become subdivided for housing tourists. Who knows, but it was interesting to speculate.

We continued our trip along the Atlantic coast through Hubbards and St Margaret's Bay, where we took a few moments to stroll along the beach at Queensland. Bob and Colleen waded briefly in the ocean and reported it to be not too cool. I was not convinced and kept my sandals firmly on my feet. It was a clear, bright day, and just watching the sunlight catching the wave tops was quite enchanting. Now we heard the call of Peggy's Cove.

The Memorial to Swiss Air Flight 111 was the first stop on the way. This is a beautiful memorial carved out of the granite that is so much part of the land-scape of this area. We spent a few minutes thinking about this tragedy, and appreciating the support the people of the region had given to the families of those on the flight. As we looked out over the very calm and sunlit sea, it was so hard to imagine the tragedy that had struck on the fateful day.

Peggy's Cove was our last stop of the day, and it began with the compulsory visit to the lighthouse. On this glorious day I looked out over smooth blue water and remembered an earlier visit with a group of Grade Five students from Ottawa. On that day in May it was cold and

windy, and it was easy to see how treacherous these rocks could be. Now the sea was as calm as it possibly could be, and the sun was out in full force. Since I had no young children to keep my eyes on, it was wonderful just to wander on the rocks and simply enjoy being there. Before we left Peggy's Cove we bought a small snack and sat in the sun to eat and enjoy the scenery. It was a really enchanted moment in time.

From this beautiful pause comes a segue to the practicalities of life: we found the washrooms, and while I would not normally discuss such things, these ones were special and need to be recorded. These are composting toilets, which is a very practical solution given the very rocky terrain and the hordes of tourists who visit this area. Through a variety of means (which are shown very graphically in the illustration below) human waste is reduced to a useful and innocuous source of fertilizer for gardens. Quite a fascinating process; or at least I thought so.

Now back to tourism. That evening we had supper at the Port Pub in Port Williams, a little way beyond Wolfville. This gastro pub prides itself in using locally produced food in season, so the menu changes according to the availability of various products. There is also a microbrewery on site where all the beer they serve is made. In keeping with the local theme, the other alcoholic beverages also come from close by. The men had the local beer while Colleen and I had a glass of Lucketts's Red Phone Box wine, an excellent choice in my mind. The Port Pub overlooks the tidal arm of the Cornwallis River, and as we ate we watched the tide come in, covering up all the red mud and silt. When we had crossed the river earlier in the evening it was just a tiny stream, but by the time we left the pub it had become a full river. This is what it means for drainage into the Midas Basis; first you see it, then you don't.

Our friends Colleen and Chris, and the dog who comes everywhere with them

The meal at the Port Pub was a lovely end to our visit with Chris and Colleen, and we look forward to seeing them again sometime in the future. It was time to start our travels again, so the following morning we jumped into our RV and left Windsor, heading towards the Grand-Pré National Historic Site. As we traveled along the narrow roads we began to recognize some of the places we had visited in our whirlwind tour of the locale over the past couple of days, which was rather enjoyable, and made us wish we could have stayed longer.

The site at Grand-Pré has very little in the way of original buildings since the area was razed by the British following the deportation of the Acadians to other parts of North America, but it has been much reconstructed. We decided to start at the Visitor Centre and almost immediately joined a guided tour of the whole site. The guide was very knowledgeable and ready with answers to all our questions, which made our visit so much more rewarding. One of the first things we were shown was a model in the display area of the dyke system, demonstrating how the Acadians were able to turn salt marsh into arable land by controlling the flow of the tidal waters in and out of the Midas Basin. These dykes were hollowed wooden logs with flap valves that would prevent sea water flowing into the fields at high tide, while holding the fresh river water in when the tide went down. A series of dykes with this integral drainage system covered a wide area of land. Over a period of three years this process changed salt marshes into arable land suitable for livestock. Hundreds of years later, traces of the original fields and dykes are still visible. It is incredible to think of the skilled engineering that created this system, which ultimately increased enormously the amount of farming land the Acadians were able to work.

The beautiful arable land from which the Acadians were expelled

Our tour guide led us outside to the present-day area of the Acadian settlement and described their way of life and the history of the area. We visited the Memorial Chapel built in the 1970s to acknowledge the expulsion of this vibrant culture, and although the chapel is not consecrated, it stands as a monument to its people. The interior is surrounded by murals that describe the history of Grand-Pré in graphic detail. We lingered long over these, absorbing the story and feeling strongly for these ordinary people disrupted and expelled through political expediency. The Acadian expulsion was a huge benefit to Louisiana and other places since the settlers brought their language, music and food, which was all incorporated into the vibrant Cajun culture that there exists today.

The Memorial Chapel and the highly romanticized statue of the fictional Evangeline

The story of Evangeline, as related in the poem by Longfellow, is fictional but it brings to light some of the issues the Acadians faced during expulsion and relocation. Families were split up and members eventually lost to each other, only to be located again by future generations long after their death. The lore of the expulsion has been handed down from generation to generation, and some of those descendants come back to visit what used to be the family home so many years ago. They appreciate the way their forefathers are acknowledged, especially with the Memorial Chapel, although a bitterness cannot help but remain.

I had heard about the Acadians and their expulsion, but really had no idea of the deeper history of these people. Learning about the impact on so many people and the continuing involvement of the descendants was quite an eye-opener, and once more reminded me of how little I know of the history of this huge country. It was altogether an interesting and informative place to visit, and although the site showed off its beautiful and well maintained gardens, it was nothing like the active farming community of the historic Acadians.

After absorbing the story of the Acadians we headed towards the Springhill Miner's Museum, a drive of a few hours by small country roads and one main highway. It was to be our last tourist stop before heading to Prince Edward Island. We have a recording of the *Ballad of Springhill* by Peggy Seeger and Ewan McColl (see p. 276), so we knew of the mine disaster there, but at this point it was just the name of a place on the map and in a song. We arrived at the museum just in time for a tour of the mine. This was a challenging time for me; my family came from the Welsh mining towns of Merthyr Vale, and I remember both my parents telling me about the mining accidents that happened in their youth. And I was in Wales myself in 1966 when the coal slag tip in Aberfan slipped, causing the death of so many children. So, going down into the mine was not easy for me because all these stories came back. However, there was little time and I had to make a decision, so I went into the mine with the other visitors. In the end, it was a positive experience, and while so much of coal mining is ugly, it was good to learn the true cost of coal.

The mine was not a pleasant place to be; it was dark and dirty and wet. Before descending we were dressed in bright yellow jackets, boots and helmets with a battery light, then we walked down a steep slope into the shaft, or adit. The slope had been modified for visitors, so it was relatively gentle compared with how it was when in use. The miners were not so lucky; in their day it was much steeper! The slope was wet and slippery, not very nice to walk down at all, and although there was a handrail to hang onto if needed, it still felt treacherous. As we went deeper into the mine the guide gave us more details. Apparently, the only reason the entrance has a very high roof is because of the depth of the seam at this point. In other areas of the mine, where the coal seam is much narrower, the roof is that much lower. In these places the miners had to crouch down to get to the coal face in order to work the seam and haul out the coal. Since this mine is very deep, the miners would take a train down the various levels to the seam they were working. But, even though they were in the mine itself, they were only paid for the time they were actually at the coal face; travel time was not included in the day's pay! In some mines this travel time could be as much as an hour each day!

In order to demonstrate what it would have been like working in the mine, the guide switched off the lighting provided for tour groups, so the only light came from our helmets. It was most unpleasant, and in an active mine the coal dust would have made it even more difficult to see and work. Then, as a final demonstration, the helmet lights were switched off and the place was densely black. It felt as if you could actually touch the darkness; as if it would contaminate you like soot. This, our guide reminded us, was what it would have been like for men trapped underground after a 'bump' or fall of rock. It was not pleasant, and as I thought of those trapped in the mines I wondered how they could have coped. There were over 500 recorded 'bumps', a sort of mini-earthquake, in this mine in the years preceding the major disaster of 1958. That disaster, and the great loss of life, resulted in the mine's closure, which was somewhat of a blessing. While this had been a really interesting tour, it was also very disturbing. My thoughts were of the miners and the conditions they worked in not all that long ago, and what should have been done to improve conditions and ensure their safety. It is unreasonable to expect mining to be truly safe, but we now know ways to mitigate some of the risks. Perhaps they were known then, but not put into practice.

The museum building had an excellent display of mining equipment, samples of coal and the surrounding matrix rocks, and on one wall was a large panel with some of the words of the *Ballad of Springhill.* Then we found something that really caught our attention: there, in a display case all by itself, was the actual manuscript of the *Ballad of Springhill* in Peggy Seeger's handwriting. Just seeing this original document brought the whole experience into focus and made us realize that Springhill, Nova Scotia was embedded somewhere deep in our past, only to be released during this visit.

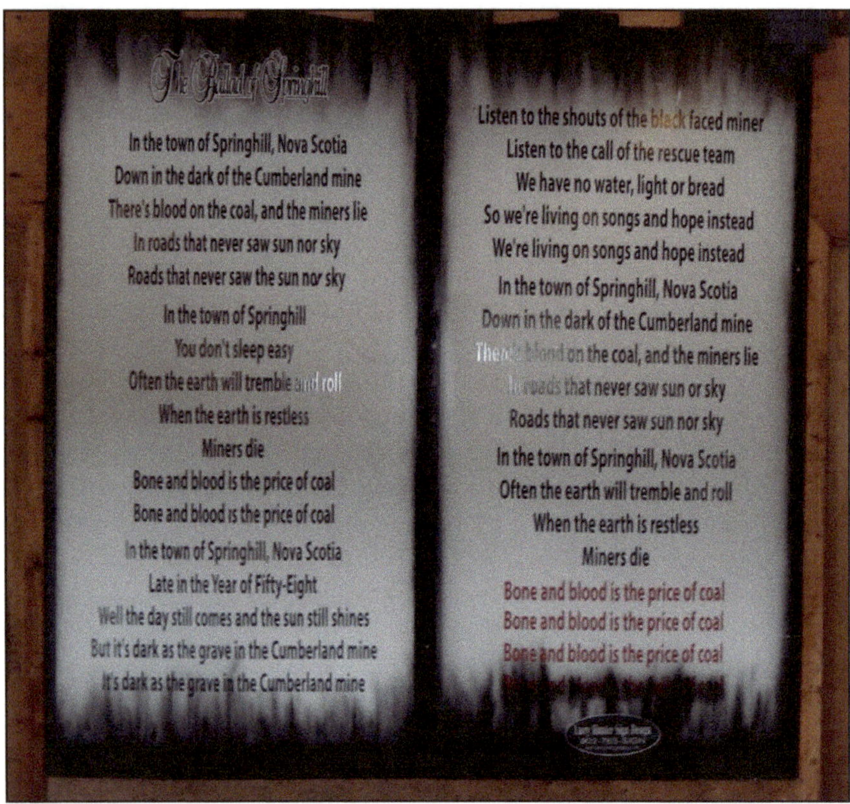

The text of The Ballad of Springhill on the wall of the exhibition building. The original manuscript is in an adjacent display case

This was a day of learning and feeling. The expulsion of the Acadians and the mining disasters in Springhill left us thinking on these things, especially the way that politics, business and power affect the lives of individuals, families and communities, usually in very negative ways. These were not happy thoughts, but things to ponder over, and perhaps mitigate—or at the very least acknowledge—similar situations occurring today. What we had seen was not isolated in history; the trends continue today in many places, and we are obliged to recognize and acknowledge them. We took these heavy thoughts away as we left Springhill, but knew that our travels in Prince Edward Island would show us a lighter side of humanity.

Our last night in Nova Scotia, before catching the ferry to Prince Edward Island, was spent at a campsite in Pictou quite near the ferry terminal. And here we had a small experience that gave thoughts on our fellow human begins a nice boost; the campsite manager wasn't in his office when we arrived, so we drove around the campground until we found an empty spot. Once settled in, Bob went back to the office and met the manager, who had just returned from dinner at his home nearby. He told Bob he knew which site he was on, because it was the only one open! We were surprised and rather thankful about that; finding another campsite late in the evening would have been a trial. Then the manager said "Merry Christmas, no charge," simply because he hadn't been there when we drove in. Talk about great customer service!

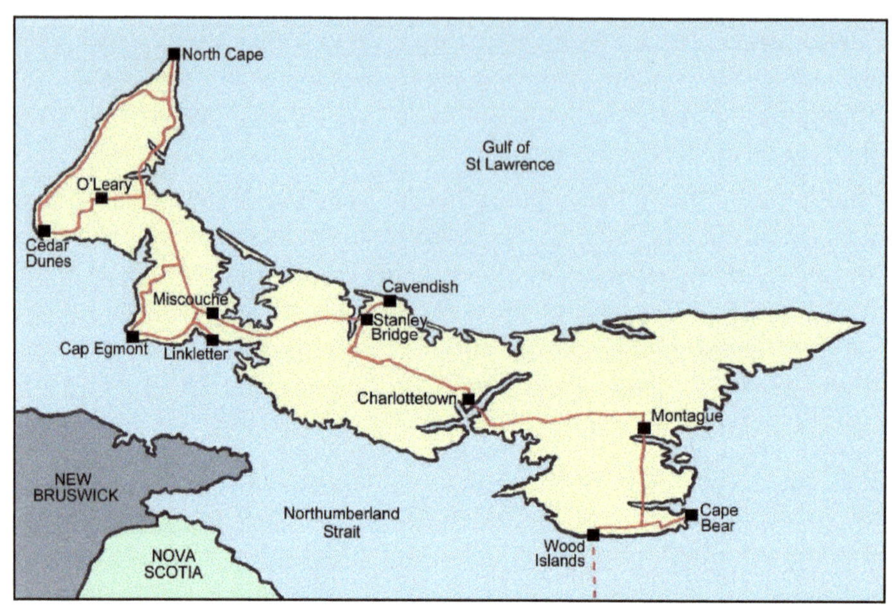

Pictou to Stanley Bridge	165km
Stanley Bridge to Cedar Dunes	199km
Cedar Dunes to Linkletter	117km
TOTAL	481km

Chapter Fifteen

Pictou to Linkletter Provincial Park

While waiting in the ferry line at Pictou we noticed a number of tour buses in the line-up, and when we boarded the vessel our little RV was parked next to one of them on the car deck. Our curiosity was satisfied once we entered the lounge; they were heading in convoy to Anne of Green Gables with their cargos of Japanese tourists. We had heard about the fascination Anne held for young Japanese women, and now we had a better understanding of what this actually meant to the tourist trade in Prince Edward Island.

Our voyage across the Northumberland Strait was beautiful and calm, with blue seas under a glorious warm sun. We spent much of the time on the upper deck just enjoying the ambience. We were reminded of the glorious weather we had experienced on the MV *Northern Ranger* so many weeks ago, and like that wonderful trip, we spent some time exchanging travel stories with other passengers.

Our first impression of Prince Edward Island and—oh, look—a lighthouse!

Once off the ferry we drove to Wood Islands Provincial Park, which was very close to the terminal and a good place to start our tourism and sort out our plans. But what is it we have about lighthouses? The first thing we visited in PEI was—naturally—the very pretty lighthouse right there in the park. All through our travels we had been reminded of the number of ships wrecked on the rugged coastlines throughout the

Maritimes, but even so we were particularly surprised at the number of shipwrecks reported off this coast. This is a sobering reminder of why Prince Edward Island has so many lighthouses. We bought a fine map in the gift shop that showed every known maritime disaster around PEI since records were kept, and it has joined our maps of other coastlines which show these somber maritime disasters.

Wood Islands lighthouse was a pretty place to start our tour of PEI

We decided to drive along the coast up the eastern side of the island, and quickly found our way to the beautiful Murray Head. Cape Bear lighthouse demanded a quick visit, but it was sad to see its need for repair. Since the automation, the preservation of these historic properties has become a big issue; they are expensive to restore and there are lots of them. Some of these icons of the coastline have been turned into private residences, some are museums, and at least one is a very nice hotel. Others are still looking for caring owners.

Cape Bear lighthouse was in poor condition and definitely needed a little TLC

I was amazed at the colour of the cliffs and the sand. I had seen pictures of the red soil of this island, of course, but to actually see it was almost shocking and nearly unbelievable. It really is red, and provides a sharp primary contrast to the sea and the vegetation. I spent time just taking in and appreciating this unique phenomenon. Now we were actually on the island, we did wonder about sailing to the Iles de la Madeleine for a couple of days, as a kind of complement to our brief visit to St Pierre. However, after some investigation of the ferry schedules, and given the few days we had allowed for PEI, we realized this would not be feasible. Besides, we had plans to visit our friends, Cheryl and Chick, in Stanley Bridge. So after our brief tour of the south-east side of the Island we drove up to Montague, and turned west.

The astonishing contrast of colours that makes the scenery of the island unique

It was wonderful being with Cheryl and Chick again, and we spent most of the time catching up with all the news. They were another of those couples who had left Ottawa and returned to their roots. Following their retirement they had moved back to PEI into the beautiful home they had built, so it was most enjoyable to be shown around. After a casual supper we spent time discussing the places we might want to visit over the next few days before returning to Stanley Bridge to attend a concert. Cheryl's niece, Catherine MacLellan, is a beautiful singer and guitarist, and this concert was to showcase her latest CD release, as well as giving us a wonderful opportunity to meet her and other family members.

As always, our plans were fluid, so before we left Stanley Bridge our friends took us on a brief tour of the area. First stop was the local farmer's market, where I bought a couple of varieties of cheese, some black garlic and a few other specialty items for our larder. (Black garlic has been fermented, which produces a sweet, tangy flavour quite different from regular garlic and complements cheese perfectly.) Looking around the market area, with all the vendors packed into a small local church, was both charming and a good opportunity to enjoy examining and buying the locally produced food.

Our first destination after the market was Green Gables—considered by some to be an absolute must—but we only saw the house from the parking lot. We are not particularly enamoured of fictional tourist destinations, and the whole industry that has grown up around the *Anne of Green Gables* stories leaves us bemused. The parking lot was packed with parked buses, not doubt some of which we had seen on the ferry; and grounds of the house were very crowded with visitors, many of whom had come from those buses. Clearly Green Gables is a very popular place to visit, but not for us. Next it was off to visit Cavendish Beach with its wonderful view of red rocks and sweeping sand. PEI's red sandstone is very soft and the coastline is eroding noticeably, thus making the cliffs hazardous. The shapes the sea carves into the rocks are quite wonderful.

Soft rocks carved by the sea

A display panel along the cliff path informed us that just offshore was the last resting place of the *Marco Polo*, the tea clipper that held the world's record for the fastest passage from the East Indies to Britain. Like so many old ships, as it aged it was demoted to lesser tasks, ending its life as a wrecked coastal freighter, so very far away from its glory days as a tea clipper. An ignominious end to a beautiful ship. We were to learn more about the *Marco Polo* on a later visit to Saint John, New Brunswick (see p. 268).

A view of Cavendish beach, one of Canada's prime bathing spots

After a little more tourism it was time to return to the house so we could reclaim our rather grubby van and go off exploring on our own. Prince Edward Island is a small province with lots of history and lots of sites to visit. Unlike many other places we have been to, the distances between interesting destinations were very short, so this part of our journey felt more like a catalogue of what to see and where to see it. I think the best way to describe it is that everything about Prince Edward Island is more *compressed.* So what follows is our very rapid exploration of new and exciting places, and some of the quite unusual tourist destinations along the way. So, here beginneth the itinerary part of our trip:

The first leg of our journey took us along the North Cape Coastal Drive, heading towards the wind farm at the very tip of the island. On our way we enjoyed our lunch and a short but relaxing beach walk at

Jacques Cartier Provincial Park., one of the very attractive parks we found dotted around the coastal landscape of the island.

The North Cape Wind Farm, partly experimental but primarily for generation

The North Cape Wind Farm sits on one of the windiest spots on the island—the whole of which seems to be very windy anyway—so it is ideally placed. We pulled into the parking lot and found ourselves a spot beside several other RVs. Right next to us was an Icon RV with Ontario licence plates and two bikes on racks. As we looked closer we noticed a hole patched with duct tape at the top corner of a panel. That patched hole—created on those long-ago Labrador roads and last seen in Twillingate—was all the evidence we needed that it was indeed the Icon owned by our friends Mike and Linda. As we walked out to the point at North Cape we kept an eye out for them; we definitely didn't want to miss them on this occasion!

Looking out over the ocean we watched a small a reef of rocks being uncovered by the tide. It was home to hundreds of birds and seals, so we just spent time observing and enjoying them. As we clambered among the rocks we soaked up the sun, appreciating the opportunity to relax and absorb the experience.

Seabirds and seals on the reef

We finally caught up with Mike and Linda in the gift shop and spent a happy hour or so sharing all the news, before they went on to their next destination. We wondered if we would see them again on this trip, but it was not to be. Then it was time to go inside the Visitor Centre of the North Cape Wind Farm and check what was on offer. The facility has a very extensive descriptive exhibition, but we found it quite disappointing. The panels are all very dense with information, most of which is very technical and in small print. I found it hard to read, and most of it was not easily understood by me as a lay person. This was a shame because I really would have liked more information in a form that could be easily comprehended. However, what I was able to glean was informative; wind energy presently meets around 18% of the island's demand for electrical power. I didn't realize it was this great a percentage, but given the prevailing winds on the island it makes good sense.

After this visit we were ready to find our way to a campsite for the night, so we left North Cape and headed down the west side of the island towards Cedar Dunes Provincial Park. As we skirted the coast we watched a wonderful vista of rain over the sea, and while enjoying the spectacle we hoped it wouldn't find us during the night! The scenery along the road were very calming; stretches of farmland, views of a very gentle sea, and then back to farmland again. Quite beautiful and very peaceful. It set the tone for our visit to this lovely place.

The campsite was sited at the back of the beach, with just a narrow strip of vegetation between us and the sand and sea. As we sat quietly in our RV we could hear the gentle sound of the waves breaking on the very red sand; a most relaxing sound and a perfect accompaniment to supper. It was a perfect evening for walking along the beach and watching the sun setting over the water. It was quite magical to see it gently and slowly disappearing. The stories of Apollo driving his chariot across the heavens and disappearing into the ocean seemed to make perfect sense, and provided more understanding of why, in earlier times, people were so focused on the return of the sun.

Sunset over the Northumberland Strait

Cedar Dunes Provincial Park boasts West Point Lighthouse, a functioning lighthouse with an attached museum, inn and restaurant. Bob had given a workshop on care of museum collections here, and had a number of stories about this experience. A visit from the 'expert' from Ottawa was a great pretext for the province's museum folk to get together socially. So his first clue that this workshop might be a bit different from the run-of-the-mill was when, chief among the workshop preparatory material, was a checklist of the meals he would like to order. Naturally, lobster was high on the list. The most memorable part of his visit was the obligatory story-telling that followed the final dinner. Around this time the Canadian Museum of Science and Technology in Ottawa had installed the original lighthouse from Cape Race, Newfoundland on a corner of St Laurent Boulevard. Bob found it easy to concoct a story with a punch line referring to the complete absence of shipwrecks on that corner since the lighthouse had been installed. So with this in mind, we found ourselves walking over to the lighthouse early the next morning.

Bob found that while the lighthouse itself had not changed, the museum displays had. He searched in vain for 'old friends' in the displays—artifacts he might recognize from his visit—but found none. The displays had all been improved and were of a much higher standard than he remembered. Although the information in the displays was specific to this lighthouse, it was also very similar to that of the other lighthouses we had visited. It must be difficult to say something unique when you have one lighthouse museum among so many (especially to people like us for whom lighthouses are some weird kind of magnet). We climbed the spiral stairs to the top of this one, of course, and found the most spectacular view. It was so clear we could see the New Brunswick shore sharply. Interestingly, even though this lighthouse is still active—now retrofitted with high tension xenon tubes—visitors are still allowed to go right up to the light. A warning is posted, advising people, obviously, not to look directly at it. It seemed odd, and at the same time exciting, to be there and to watch the light rotate as the timed flashes went out across the ocean.

Another lighthouse. They are of a fairly standard pattern and they become indistinguishable

Our next stop on our PEI explorations was a visit to the Potato Museum in O'Leary. And, yes, we thought it was a good joke; after all we knew all about potatoes, didn't we? We had visited the Hammer

Museum in Haines, Alaska, and thought we knew all about hammers, so really a potato museum in PEI did not seem all that far-fetched, so off we went. As with the Hammer Museum, we were quickly disabused of all our preconceptions and found a most interesting display, showing many different types of equipment of all periods, diseases of the potato in graphic detail, and its very intricate and colourful history. Who knew the potato originated in the New World and was brought back to Europe by the Spaniards, who had seen how the Incas used them? To our surprise, when spuds first came to Europe in the 16th century they were used as animal feed. I had never thought of how difficult it had been to accept the humble potato as a good food. The other surprising piece of information was the high Vitamin C content, and the effective use of potatoes in preventing scurvy during long sea voyages. I knew limes were used by the British Navy in order to prevent this vitamin deficiency disease, but didn't realize that potatoes would be as effective. It gave me more respect for this useful tuber.

The Potato Museum's unique icon, complete with eyes

It was now lunchtime, so before leaving the museum we decided to eat in the cafeteria. Naturally, it was a menu based on potatoes, so of course we had to try the offerings! We went for the all-dressed baked potato. This was not your average potato, but one loaded with bacon, peppers, cheese, sour cream and goodness know what else. Quite delicious and a full meal all on its own. Then, of course, we had to choose the seaweed pie for dessert! This sounded weird to us, but had to be tried. Basically, it is angel food cake with a layer of seaweed mousse and whipped cream on top. Since there was no seaweed taste we asked the server where the seaweed might be hidden in the dessert. She told us that Irish moss (seaweed) had been processed and used as the thickening agent in the mousse, rather like an agar. It had no flavour, which I think was probably a very good thing. All in all, the Potato Museum was a really wonderful and unexpected place to visit. It is one of those crazy places you often don't think of visiting, and I for one am glad I did. But, how about that all-dressed potato!

In early January 2014, being in desperate need of sun and warm weather, we had visited Las Vegas to watch curling. (And yes, we recognize the irony of this.) However, we did take the opportunity to visit Death Valley in California, and during our travels there we came across a signpost describing a bottle house in a town called Rhyolite (above). We had no idea what this was until we discovered, in this mining ghost town, was a house built of a variety of glass bottles held in place with cement. A most unusual sight. With this in mind, an advertisement in the tourist information for bottle houses at Cap Egmont on the south coast had caught our eye. So we thought it would be interesting to compare the two venues.

Without doubt, the houses at Cap Egmont were much more attractive than the one we had seen earlier in the year. The house in Rhyolite was built mainly with bottles of one or two colours and essentially just stuck in the concrete as they came. However, the designs we saw here in PEI were intricately created by the differing colours and shapes of the bottles. When inside the houses it was difficult to make out the patterns, but when looking at them from the outside the designs became clear. The *pièce de résistance* is perhaps the Chapel. It is set up like a proper place of worship with pews built entirely out of bottles and cement, and even the altar has been done in the same style. Bizarre yes, and beautiful too, and with all the motifs one expects in a small family chapel. The total experience of this strange place came as a real surprise, and it was one of those visits that create some great memories. After finishing our tour of the buildings we went to the gift shop and learned the tale of the houses and a brief history the builder.

The beautiful use of multicoloured bottles. On the right one of the houses, and below the interior of the chapel

The houses were built over many years by Edouard Arsenault, who was a lighthouse keeper with a quirky sense of humour. In all, he used over 25,000 bottles in creating a number of wonderful structures.

At some point he started collecting bottles of every shape and size, and when he had enough he started to build a single house, holding the bottles together with concrete. Once people heard what he was doing they started to donate all kinds of bottles for the project; the original recycling opportunity. He created a number of buildings over the years, situated in a lovely garden, and he also built a scale model of the lighthouse he had lived and worked in for so long. Soon after his death the houses were very carefully taken apart and then rebuilt because there was a concern over the safety and integrity of the original structures. The land was unstable and the foundations had started to shift. Very many photographs and careful measurements ensured that the reconstructed buildings were very close to original. In fact, all the original bottles were reused and the only addition was new concrete. A landscaper was also brought in to improve the setting of the houses and the general area, which has resulted in visitors being able to stroll through a very peaceful and beautiful landscape. At one point we just sat quietly on a bench and enjoyed the calm this lovely place provided. We were left with an impression of contrast: the bottle house in Rhyolite had actually been lived in for many years, whereas these attractive structures that Arsenault had built were purely for show.

After our visit to Grand-Pré in Nova Scotia, we were curious to visit the Acadian Museum of Prince Edward Island in Miscouch to learn some of the history of the Acadians in this little island. The museum was just a few kilometres down the road, so we just dropped in, finally beginning to grasp just how small PEI actually is. Like most other museum visits we started with a film that gave a brief historical outline, from the original settlers arriving from France in the early 18th century, through the deportation of the Acadians in the late 18th century, and the rejuvenation of the culture since then. The exhibition was fascinating, and while it reiterated much of what we had already learned, it provided some specific local information.

One of the more surprising facts was the difficulty the Acadians had encountered in maintaining their language in English-speaking PEI. We had found that French was alive and well in parts of Cape Breton, particularly in Chéticamp where we had stopped for a coffee. However, now the schools in PEI are stressing Acadian French, and one can only hope this will have long-term success. If Cape Breton can bring back Gaelic, then there is hope for PEI to maintain its French.

It had been a very busy day, with much food for thought, so we were happy to find Linkletter Provincial Park, another beautiful location right on the ocean and only a few minutes away from the museum. However, the rain we had run away from the day before now caught up with us; not too much of a concern, all snug and warm in our vehicle, but we did feel for those hardy souls out there in tents. We have spent many an outdoor camping night sleeping (or not) while listening to the rain coming down on the canvas, so as thunder rumbled all around us and the wind blew we were thankful to have an impermeable roof over our heads. Fortunately for our tourism plans, the storm blew over during the night, and we woke to calmer weather and the opportunity to explore both Summerside, the island's second largest city, and Charlottetown the capital.

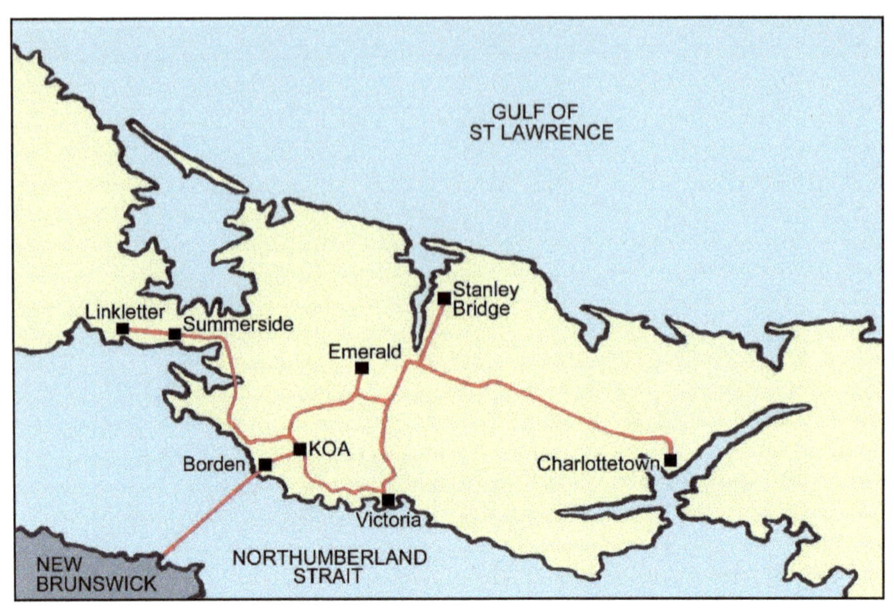

Linkletter to Stanley Bridge	117km
Stanley Bridge to Borden	128km
TOTAL	245km

Chapter Sixteen

Linkletter Provincial Park to Borden

This was the start of a very ambitious day of tourism. Our planned destination was Summerside, only a very short distance away from Linkletter. As we traveled we began to realize that by now we had driven a significant portion of the roads of Prince Edward Island, and that they have their own unique characteristics. We were often driving over what looked like a chequerboard gone wrong, with the pink road-bed overlaid with black squares, rectangles and circles of asphalt. And in some minor roads we even encountered our good friend and traveling companion, gravel. It was actually quite charming in its way!

We parked the RV next to the Summerside Visitor Information Centre, and here we met one of the most helpful people in the system. This official took his time to describe all the attractions he could, and by the time he had finished, the map he provided was marked with so many circles and arrows and lines and descriptions that we thought it would take us days to do it all. So, armed with our much-annotated map we went first to the Bishop's Machine Shop.

This was a fascinating place to visit, and a magnet for all metalworking machine aficionados. The shop in all its iterations had been in continuous use since the 1880s, first as a foundry and then, when the foundry moved next door, as a machine shop. We looked into the building next door first, and discovered it was now a flea market, and prior to that, had been a daycare. Nothing was left to signify its history as an important part of the industrial infrastructure of Summerside. The machine shop, on the other hand, was beautifully preserved. Its last owner had retired from business in the 1970s, but continued to use the machine tools until a couple of years before his death in the late 1990s. All the equipment had been carefully cleaned and coated in oil for protection, so when we saw the place everything was in immaculate condition. The title to the property had been was transferred to the city sometime after the owner's death, and the site maintained as a wonderful example of late 19th and early 20th century metalworking practice. All the machines in the entire shop are run by belt drives, initially by a steam engine and then more recently by electricity. There are lathes, shapers, milling machines, a very old band-saw, and many other machine tools, all in beautiful condition. The belt drive system itself is a marvel of ingenuity; a wonderful microcosm of an era. We spent about an hour looking at everything and talking with the student guide. He was very knowledgeable about the shop and took great delight in our interest, pointing out things he thought important, and which without his guidance we might have missed.

A wonderful array of machine tools, all run from belt drives along the ceiling

After almost an hour we headed towards the Fox Museum, recommended and well-circled by the staff member in the Visitor Centre, and heartily endorsed by our friendly student. We seem to like finding odd museums to visit. We have visited many of the grand houses of various eras, and have learned a great deal of history from them, but after a while they seem to run into one another and begin to look the same. Even so, we do understand they really are varied and important to the particular cultural and social history of the places we visit. But museums like the Hammer Museum in Haines, Alaska or the Potato

Museum here in PEI, or even the Banff History Museum in British Columbia stand out in showing unusual aspects of a place. The Fox Museum was another one of these. After all, who knew there was a booming fox fur industry here in the first part of the 20th century? We certainly didn't.

Fox furs laid out so museum visitors can feel their texture.

This little exhibition was located in the old Armoury building and occupying just the first floor. The history of the fur industry was outlined, from the selective breeding of foxes to ensure the fashionable colours of fur, to the industrial nature of the farming. It seems this was a very lucrative business, and everybody wanted in on the action. Many fortunes were made during this period, and subsequently lost towards the end of the industry as the demand for fox fur decreased. One of the panels showed a very fancy Packard saloon, bought by one of the wealthier fox breeders in the 1920s with the astonishing price tag of one third of a breeding pair of foxes! The industry lasted only about 50 years before the market became saturated and tastes changed, so those interested in the fur business moved on to other, more fashionable types of fur or simply went under. This was a fascinating little exhibition, and we enjoyed learning about an industry we hadn't dreamed existed. However, the displays did not discuss any aspects of the slaughter of the livestock, or the skills needed in preparation of the skins to produce the perfect furs for the business. Perhaps this was done to avoid offending visitors' sensibilities, but we both thought it would have been of interest to at least read a little about these very important skills.

A brief exploration of the upper floor of the Armory building revealed an exhibition paying homage to the firefighters of the area. This pictorial history of firefighting was seen through the lenses of photographers who had chronicled the many fires that volunteers had dealt with over the history of Summerside. In addition to the photographs around the walls, there were a few exhibits in the centre of the room, one of which was a two-gallon leather bucket. Each household was required to have one, so when fire erupted this item would play an important role in the bucket brigade, the original method of fighting fires. Each bucket was labeled with the owner's name so once the fire was out, buckets could be returned to their rightful place. Needless to say, this was not the most efficient way of fire-fighting, so very soon better and more efficient ways were found. We were impressed with the pictures of early fire engines, particularly one of a steam fire engine, and another of the manual fire pump that predated it. We hoped these more 'modern' fire engines were a little more successful than the bucket brigade. I came away from this exhibition understanding that in a town built mainly of wood, the fire department plays a significant role. Today, with sprinklers and smoke detectors, we tend to forget the very real danger fire poses to people and property.

After our very busy and thought-provoking morning we needed to pause and regroup. The College of Pipers in Summerside is an important venue in maintaining and encouraging the traditional music of Scotland and Ireland. Many of families in PEI are descended from settlers of both places, and their musical traditions—piping, harp playing, songs and dances—all play an important part in the culture of this place. So it made sense, especially given Bob's interest in music and musicology and his tenuous Scottish heritage, that we took advantage of a visit. We had arrived after the close of the school year, so there were no performances or programs available. However, a short video of a concert presented by the students gave us a taste of the performances they staged regularly.

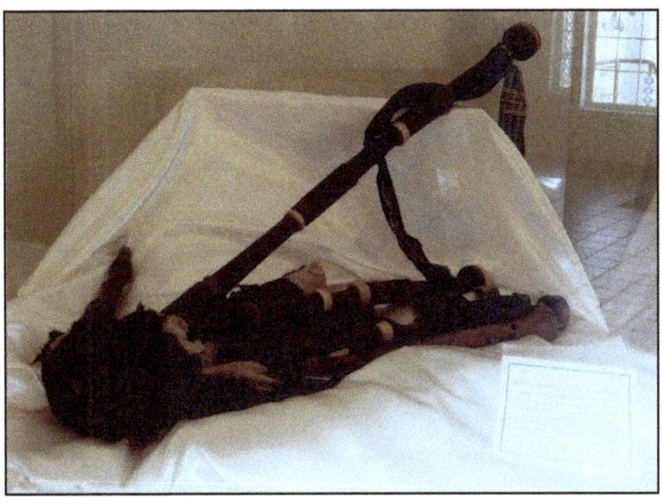

Bagpipes played at Culloden, photographed with some difficulty through their display case

While looking around the foyer we noticed an ancient set of bagpipes in a display case, and were extremely surprised to learn that these pipes were actually played at the Battle of Culloden. This was the final confrontation of the Jacobite Rising of 1745, when the army of Prince Charles Stuart was beaten by the Duke of Cumberland on behalf of the English Crown. Below the display case was an article from the *Ottawa Journal*, of June 14, 1952 that outlined in great detail the clear provenance of the pipes. We were entranced by the thought of the journey these pipes had taken; from Culloden to Ottawa to Prince Edward Island and the College of Pipers. This was a wonderful piece of living history and one we hardly expected to find. It was a great conclusion to our explorations in Sunnyside.

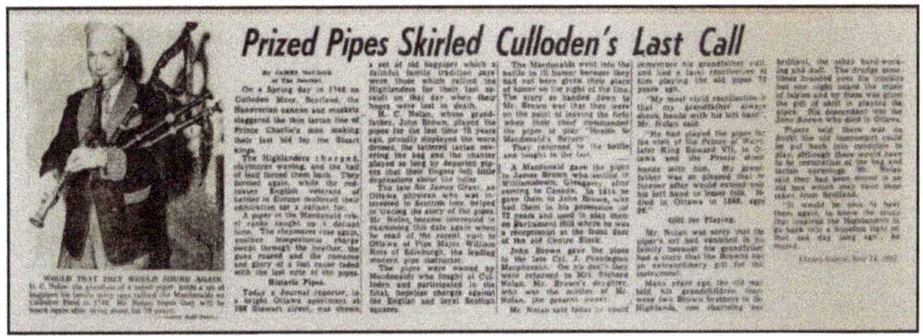

Prized Pipes Skirled Culloden's Last Call

Our helpful person in the Summerside Information Centre had told us of a ceilidh that night in Emerald, a small town in the middle of the island. We decided we must take in such an important feature of Prince Edward Island entertainment, so after checking into the KOA campsite near Borden for that night, we turned around and headed up to Emerald, by way of a little detour to admire the various small towns along the Northumberland Strait seashore, particularly Victoria. One particular monument caught our eye; a church steeple painted in red and white stripes, as if there weren't enough lighthouses in that livery already!

Just for a change, it isn't a lighthouse

Close to Emerald we encountered one short section of gravel road, and thankfully found it was a very good one, so neither we nor the vehicle complained about it. We made our way to the Community Centre where the ceilidh was to be held, and then a whole new world opened up. It was clear when we walked in that this was a community event and that everyone knew everyone else. The bar and the kitchen were run by volunteers, which gave a very homely and local feel to the event. We were there early, or so we thought, but it looked as if the whole community was there as well. We had decided to have our supper here before the start of the ceilidh, and as we waited in line, firstly for tickets and then to place our order, we found that everybody else was doing the same thing. The dining room filled up very quickly, and many diners were taking their meals into the adjoining concert hall. It was clear this overflow was a common practice given the limited number of tables available. After we ordered our meals we were assigned a number and were told it would be called when the food was ready! A number also appeared on screens in the lounge and concert hall, just in case you happened to be out of earshot when they called. So we sat in the lounge area, off to one side of the dining room, until our number was called. It was a long wait, since the meals were cooked individually by just two or three people in the kitchen. The wait was made more interesting when we were joined by a mother and her son. She was visiting him from England, as he had settled here in PEI. We had a long conversation with both of them, which helped pass the time until our meal was ready. The food was plain but tasty and more than made up for the wait. The timing was perfect because just as we finished eating we could hear the musicians preparing for the show.

The hall was already full for this obviously popular event, but we managed to find seats. This particular ceilidh had been recommended by the tourism staffer in Summerside because he thought Courtney Hogan, the fiddle player, was particularly good. We agreed with him. The concert was wonderfully accomplished, and the musicians played a wide range of music, from reels and jigs to country to Elvis and everything in between. What a show! At one point two sisters came onto the stage and performed several intricate step dances. We had heard of the popularity of step dancing but hadn't really seen much of it. The sisters had won several step dancing competitions throughout the province; it showed. They were very accomplished, and we really enjoyed watching them. It was also interesting to observe the audience's reaction, as it was obvious the girls were well known in the community and had a lot of local support.

Courtney Hogan's 2-CD set Swinging on a Note, *a superb compendium of her talent*

While all this was underway, supper was still being served. Once in a while the screen beside the stage would flash up a number, and so patrons waiting for their food hurried out to the serving counter to collect their meals and bring them back to the hall. The few tables at the back of the room proved very helpful for these hungry diners. It was all very casual and very much a family affair. As with most concerts of this kind, there was a CD sale during intermission, so of course we bought one, and naturally asked Courtney Hogan to sign it. We spent many happy hours listening to this recording during the rest of our travels.

Once the ceilidh was over we made our way back to our campsite. As we thought about all we had seen and done we realized that Prince Edward Island may be small, but it has so much to offer. It has a very different nature, distinct from all those big city attractions and the wild outdoors we are so used to. It is a gentle place, warm, friendly, densely packed and full of wonderful and charming surprises.

The next day would be our last for exploring the island and also close to the end of this year's adventures. We had to head back to our friends in Stanley Bridge so as to be in good time for the concert that evening. But first, Charlottetown was on the agenda. We found our way to the capital of Prince Edward Island by mid-morning, parked the van in a makeshift parking lot right on the waterfront, and headed straight for the tourist centre where we once again met very helpful staff. The excellent information we received set us up for a good day of tourism.

Our first stop of the day was right there on the wharf. Some Tall Ships were in dock, four of them, plus a 'pirate ship' that was giving short trips into the harbour and firing off its guns at regular intervals. We boarded one of the ships and found it was actually out of Ottawa, and spent its winters docked in the Rideau Canal near the Chateau Laurier! Almost in our backyard. This particular ship was steel-hulled, with both sails and engine, and had been commissioned by a businessman for his family's use in the Mediterranean during the summer, when he would find time to fly over and visit. Now the ship is used in a youth program associated with the Tall Ships. These young people go to sea and learn how to navigate under sail, and for some it even counts as a high school credit. I could wish I had had that option as teenager; it would have been hard work, but so much fun. We spent some time wandering around the ship and then walked along the dock to view the other sailing vessels there. It seemed that every tourist in Charlottetown had chosen just that moment to board the vessels, so we decided to just enjoy the craft from a distance. The 'pirate ship' was very active in offering tours in the harbour, and every so often we would hear the crew firing the cannons across the water. It made for some startling moments until we realized what was happening. It was a wonder they had got a permit for firing their black powder around tourists!

Sailing ships in the Charlottetown harbour

On the wharf beside the tall ships was an interesting looking warehouse building that was begging us to go in and see what it had to offer. Inside were a number of stalls selling crafts and tourist items, one of which offered jams and relishes. After we tested a couple of them we bought a few jars to bring back to Ottawa. We kept them for a special time and thoroughly enjoyed them over the Christmas season.

Prince Edward Island was celebrating the 150th anniversary of the Charlottetown Conference, when delegates met to outline what would one day become Canada. There were entertainments in a park near the harbour, which we watched for a short while before walking on. We came across a spectacular celebratory stone carving, an intricately formed sculpture of the participants at that defining moment in Canadian history.

150th anniversary sculpture in red sandstone

Because of this momentous celebration, an essential visit was to Province House, built in 1847. Today, the building serves as the home of the PEI Legislature. As we walked toward Province House we passed St Dunstan's Cathedral, a lovely looking building which enticed us to pause and look inside. It was quite beautiful and peaceful, with some lovely stained glass windows, and we spent a little time looking around and enjoying the quietness of the place. Then it was on to Province House and the creation of Confederation.

A pleasant pause in the peace of St Dunstan's

It seems to be a routine today that as soon as you enter a historic building you watch a movie. Today was no different. The movie was all about the 1864 meeting between the Maritime Premiers and politicians from Upper Canada. It was well acted and very authentically staged, and set the scene for both of us, as our knowledge of the details of that important meeting were sketchy. So I, for one, really appreciated having the opportunity to learn much more about this key step in recent Canadian history. After the movie we visited the rest of the building, and were able to visit the actual rooms where these important meetings were held. Like interiors everywhere, the décor and furnishings had changed over time, but the location has now been restored to reflect the way it was in the 1860s. Standing in that room it was easy to imagine how it must have been during that critical period. It was really fascinating to see the actual place where the idea of Confederation was conceived, and ultimately created just a few years later.

After we left Province House we still had some time in Charlottetown so we wandered about the city, eventually coming across Cows, reputedly the best ice cream in town or, as the boast was, in the entire world. Naturally, we went in and bought a small dish, and I am happy to report that it was quite delicious. Is it the best? In the whole world? I don't know, but on that rather warm day in Charlottetown, it certainly rated extremely high on the list.

For our final historical exploration we visited a stately house with a somewhat different history. This house had been constructed for a shipbuilder who went bankrupt a few years later, so it passed on to another owner, and eventually became a residence for nurses from the local hospital. Finally, the house was renovated to the earlier period of its life, and is now open to the public. It was a rather attractive building, and given my background as a nurse, I enjoyed thinking about all those nurses who had lived there, and wondered about the stories they might have had to tell.

Charlottetown proved to be a fine end to our tourism on the island, but we wished there had been time for so much more. Like the rest of PEI, attractions are many and packed tightly in the capital. We had enjoyed our exploration of this delightful island and wished we could have stayed longer, but we knew it was getting close to that time when we needed to be back home in Ottawa.

We drove back again to Stanley Bridge and our friends. After giving the RV a good shampoo and wash on the outside, and a good cleaning within (it really needed it by now) the four of us drove back into Charlottetown and sat down in a local pub/restaurant for supper. There we met a number of Cheryl's family members and had a delightful time chatting with them and getting to know them better. After supper the entire family group set off to the theatre where Cheryl's niece, Catherine MacLellan was playing. The very enjoyable concert proved to be a very contrasting experience to the ceilidh we had attended in Emerald. But there was still that strong feeling of this being a family affair, with many kin and friends coming out to support their musician. The musicianship was first class, and Catherine had assembled some top rate players to support her. Her partner Chris Gauthier is a brilliant guitarist, and a great accompanist for Catherine, while the rest of the crew were equally accomplished. She is both singer and songwriter, and almost all the songs were her own compositions. It was a most successful evening and we topped it off by buying one of her CDs, signed of course, and added that to our collection of traveling music. This CD later won a Juno Award.

The Raven's Sun, *Catherine MacLellan's CD that we bought after the concert*

After this late night in Charlottetown we had a slow morning; I spent extra time sleeping while Bob chatted with our friends. It was now time to say farewell to Prince Edward Island and head towards New Brunswick via the Confederation Bridge, and onwards to our next rendezvous in Saint John. So after our lazy morning we said goodbye to our friends, left Stanley Bridge and headed westward, back to the mainland of Canada. When we had boarded the ferry to PEI there were no ferry fees, but as we approached the Bridge, we had to pay to leave the island. It was very tempting to turn around and stay!

As we crossed this immense bridge we realized what a phenomenal structure it is. A couple of years ago we had driven across the causeway over Lake Pontchartrain in Louisiana, and had thought that pretty spectacular, but really it is merely low and very long. The Confederation Bridge is much more spectacular, and I was glad to have seen it and driven across it. Once in New Brunswick we made a brief stop at the Visitors Centre to photograph the bridge for our records. It really is a magnificent piece of engineering.

Bridge comparisons

The Confederation Bridge viewed from the New Brunswick side

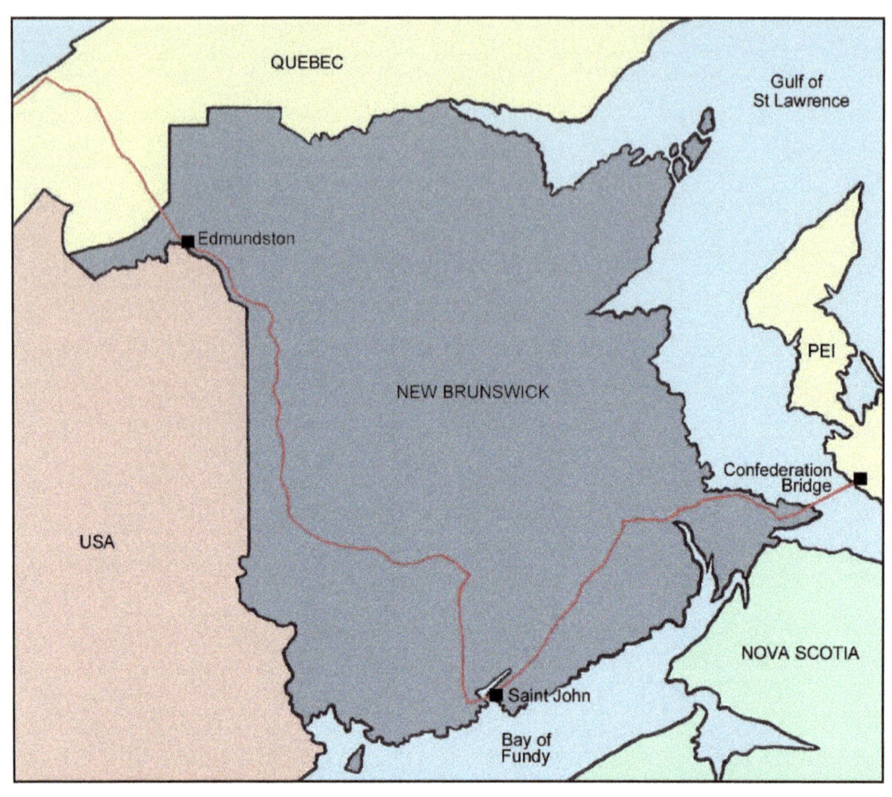

Stanley Bridge to Saint John		420km
Saint John to Quebec City		698km
Quebec City to Ottawa		428km
	TOTAL	1546km

Chapter Seventeen

Borden to Ottawa

This was the final leg of our long journey, and home was beginning to call. It had been a wonderful adventure, but it was coming to a close. Though not before visiting our friends, Pat and Ken, in Saint John, New Brunswick. So, having crossed the Confederation Bridge we headed directly to their home on the outskirts of Saint John, with its stunning view over the Kennebecasis River. Once more we were able to park the vehicle in a driveway and hook up to our host's utilities. This was one thing we had enjoyed with all our visits: being with friends yet still having one's own space. I am sure it makes us better visitors and hopefully better company.

We arrived in the late afternoon and had a fine time chatting and catching up with all the news. Bob and Ken spent a happy hour or so just telling stories, while Pat and I simply talked. We were also planning for the following day when Bob and I would go into Saint John to explore the city; just roaming around the centre of town, and seeing what we could see. So after breakfast Pat gave us a mini tour of the neighbourhood, where we encountered some beautiful seascapes, which almost tempted us to move to this lovely area. Then she dropped us off in the centre of town and left us to explore.

Once in Saint John we found the Tourist Information Office, and armed with maps of the city and the province, we were on our way. Saint John holds an annual sculpture competition where sculptors from all over the world compete for a chance to come here to sculpt in stone and have their works exhibited. We were lucky enough to be there for this competition. Each sculptor is issued with a block of stone, and the works produced during the competition are placed in various towns throughout New Brunswick. This year there were eight sculptors working in outdoor studios at the dockside, with several sculptures in the process of being carved. This innovative concept is supported by some of the big industries of the area, as well as the municipalities where the sculptures will finally be placed. The outlay to the chosen towns is much less than the true cost of the sculptures because of this community support.

No hammers and chisels here; these people are equipped with serious power tools

It was fascinating to walk around the site and watch the men and women working on their pieces, and to note the tools they were using. There was very little chipping at their blocks of stone using the traditional hammer and chisel, but rather the use of power tools, which are much more efficient at removing material and finding the image hidden in it. As we left the site we picked up a brochure that described a 'sculpture walk'. This was intriguing. There were ten sites in the city where public sculptures could be seen, and we thought this would be a great way to visit the core of the city and see some interesting art as we did so.

On our way up King Street, away from the harbour, we heard bagpipes in the distance, and before we knew it we were watching a Labour Day parade. As we walked slowly up King Street the parade marched down. It was enjoyable to see all the participants in the cavalcade obviously having fun on a warm September day.

Bagpipes seem to follow us

Eventually, we came upon the Saint John Market, the first stop on our sculpture walk. This is the oldest continuous farmer's market in Canada, with a charter dating from 1785. The present building houses a covered market with every kind of stall you can imagine, all under a very attractive roof that resembles an upturned boat. There were the usual fruit and vegetable stalls of markets one finds everywhere, meat and fish stalls, and the odd beer stall as well. Then came the paintings and postcards, the handicrafts, the jewellery, the clothing, and so on. Quite the eclectic mix and wonderful to see. After a great deal of searching, and vainly questioning a few natives, we found the piece of sculpture described in the brochure. It was high up on the outside wall of the building and not that easy to see from ground level. Once we located this piece we enjoyed showing it to a couple of locals who had no idea of where or what it was. Sometimes it takes tourists to remind residents of the wonderful things to see in their cities, as we have found in our native Ottawa.

Inside, the market was an absolute riot of colour, sound and smell

Our next stop took us to the Aliant Building and then to the Saint John Art Centre. The artworks we were looking for proved easy to find and were quite attractive. As we walked back down towards the harbour (the hills in Saint John are quite steep) we found several more of the sculptures and appreciated this very different way of exploring a city. The search led us into Market Square where we found most of the other works, as well as some interesting stores. We were also reminded of the story of the *Marco Polo* and its sad demise when we came across a model of it, just above the atrium of the square.

A huge model of the Marco Polo, *commemorating the building of the ship in Saint John in 1851*

After our adventures searching out all that public art, we decided to take a walk along Water Street, which runs along the docks. This was a real mix of old and new, and it was interesting to note how the new and old buildings seemed to complement each other without compromising the actual street scene. Along the way we paused by a number of informative historical plaques. I had no idea the first steam foghorn had been designed and used in Saint John in 1859. We could appreciate why; as we were walking around the fog began to come down in the harbour, hence the importance of developing a warning system.

It's not surprising that Saint John is the birthplace of the foghorn

And who knew the first vessel in the world propelled by a compound steam engine was the *Reindeer*, launched in 1845! We enjoyed the contrast of streetscapes; there were rows of tall warehouses and commercial buildings, while only one street over we came across some really cute little houses perched on the rock.

Very desirable properties overlooking the harbour

Tall red brick commercial buildings in the harbour area

After a gentle ramble through the lower town, admiring the street scenes and varied architecture, it was time to find a taxi and make our way back to Pat and Ken and supper.

The evening was spent talking and laughing over a lovely supper of roast beef accompanied by Ken's homemade wine, and as the red wine flowed so did the stories. It was a wonderful way to end our visit to New Brunswick and to signal the close of our maritime adventure. We had left Ottawa in July and now it was September and we needed to get back. For us, six weeks was a long time to be away, and now our day-to-day life was coming back to haunt us in the form of e-mails from family, friends and coworkers. So, much as we would have liked to have extended our stay and see more in Saint John, it really was time to head west for home.

After breakfast we said goodbye and started back. This part of New Brunswick is known for its fog, as we had seen the day before, and this day was no exception. The first part of the trip was quite foggy, but gradually as we made our way inland it dissipated, which made driving a little better. We followed the Saint John River north, passed through Edmundston, and crossed the Quebec border. Unfortunately, the good driving conditions changed after lunch, as Bob found out; construction and bad roads seemed to be his lot in life! Roadworks before Rivière-du-Loup made the driving painful. We turned west at Rivière-du-Loup and stopped that night in a KOA just outside Quebec City at about 5:30 Atlantic Time, or 4:30 Eastern Time, which was not a bad day of driving, given the conditions.

The following day saw us home in Ottawa in a little under five hours, and as we relaxed in our living room after six weeks on the road we were able to reflect on this trip.

This journey to the north and east was very different from our previous trip, north and west. The trip to Inuvik and through Alaska had introduced us to so many varied landscapes, communities and experiences. Because it was so much further north, and included crossing the Arctic Circle, we had driven through very diverse terrains and had encountered a wider variety of landscapes. Even though we had spent limited time on or near the coastlines of the north and west, we had become more aware of the impact of climate and terrain on the peoples of those areas. This time, driving east and some distance north, and traveling across islands and beside seashores, we were much more conscious of the sea and its effect on populations; how changes in shipbuilding, exploration and the netting of the sea's bounty affected the inhabitants of these coastlines. The indigenous populations, the early Norse settlers, and all those who came after from all parts of Europe: all were deeply affected by the sea.

The landscapes and seascapes created fascinating contrasts. The rugged-ness of Labrador and Newfoundland, the slightly softer mountains of Cape Breton, the change again to the softer and more agricultural aspect of Nova Scotia, and finally the rounded gentleness of Prince Edward Island, all had an impact on us. While I found the mountains and barrens of Labrador and Newfoundland quite beautiful, I was also conscious of the harshness and hardness of those places, and found myself longing for softer landscapes. Cape Breton had some of the most glorious views—the Gulf of St Lawrence viewed from the Highlands was something to behold—and while the mountains were somewhat less harsh than those in Labrador, I pined for a flatter landscape to rest my eyes upon. As we crossed from Cape Breton into Nova Scotia with its more level places, I felt myself relaxing and enjoying longer vistas and the denser farmland. To be sure, there were areas, especially on the coastline, where the rocks showed themselves in all their harshness, but there still was a much softer feel to the countryside. Finally, arriving in Prince Edward Island, the whole landscape changed yet again. Yes, the coastline is still quite rocky and it has a long history of shipwrecks, but away from the coast it is a much more open, gentle and rolling landscape. Wide open spaces of farmland were divided into manageable sized fields, and its scale made it feel gentler and kinder.

I was surprised at my own reaction to the various landscapes, and I have come to the conclusion that while I admire the crags of mountains and the harshness of a rocky seacoast, I really prefer the lush, gentle places with long horizons unbroken by mountains, with a variety of vegetation from grasslands to trees to forests. I had noticed this desire a little on our previous trip, when my relief at coming out of the mount-ains of British Columbia and Alberta was reinforced by finally seeing the long horizons of the prairies. Will this prevent me from going into the mountains again? Of course not, but living in close proximity to mountains is unlikely to be in my future. I have finally realized that I need those open vistas for my own wellbeing. Yes, I live in a city, but as I reflect on this, I know how often I travel out to the countryside, and how important it is for me to have greenspace, no matter how small, around me. I don't think I could ever happily live in the heart of a city with very little green around me, nor could I live happily among mountains.

Journeys are about exploring both the world and oneself, and these two long trips to all three sides of this huge country have been just that. Bob and I have learned so much about Canada in all its width and depth, and about ourselves as well. We still reminisce over all our travels in close proximity, and the comfort of our relationship with each other and the diverse landscapes of our home. And while we reminisce, we also find ourselves thinking and planning for the next great adventure, and wonder where it will take.

This is a story to be continued.

Resources

Barclay, Janet, *Points North and West* (Ottawa: Loose Cannon Press, 2014) ISBN 978-0-9936881-3-3

Battle Harbour
http://www.battleharbour.com/

Budgell, Anne, *Dear Everybody,* (Portugal Cove/St Philip's, NL: Boulder Publications, 2013) ISBN 978-1-927099-17-9

French Shore Tapestry
http://www.frenchshoretapestry.com/en/intro.asp

Kunz, Keneva (translator), *The Vinland Sagas* (London, UK: Penguin Classics, 1997) ISBN 978-0-140-44776-7

Nunutsiavut Marine
http://www.labradorferry.ca/

Tourism Newfoundland and Labrador
http://www.newfoundlandlabrador.com/

Tourism Nova Scotia
http://www.novascotia.com/

Tourism New Brunswick
http://www. toursimnewbrunswick.ca /

Tourism Prince Edward Island
http://www.tourismpei.com/index.php3

Wilfred Grenfell Historic Properties
http://grenfell-properties.com/

I'se the B'y

I'se the b'y that builds the boat
And I'se the b'y that sails her
I'se the b'y that catches the fish
And takes 'em home to Liza

[chorus]

Hip your partner Sally Thibeau
Hip your partner Sally Brown
Fogo, Twillingate, Morton's Harbour
All around the circle

Sods and rinds to cover the flake
Cake and tea for supper
Codfish in the spring of the year
Fried in maggoty butter

[chorus]

I don't want your maggoty fish
That's no good for a winter
I can get much better than that
Down in Bonavista

[chorus]

I took Liza to a dance
Faith but she could travel
And every step that she did take
Was up to her knees in gravel

[chorus]

I'se the b'y that builds the boat
And I'se the b'y that sails her
I'se the b'y that catches the fish
And takes 'em home to Liza

The Ballad of Springhill

In the town of Springhill, Nova Scotia,
Down in the dark of the Cumberland Mine,
There's blood on the coal,
And the miners lie,
In roads that never saw sun or sky,
Roads that never saw sun or sky.

In the town of Springhill you don't sleep easy,
Often the earth will tremble and roll,
When the earth is restless miners die,
Bone and blood is the price of coal,
Bone and blood is the price of coal.

In the town of Springhill, Nova Scotia,
Late in the year of fifty-eight,
The day still comes and the sun still shines,
But it's dark as the grave in the Cumberland Mine,
Dark as the grave in the Cumberland Mine.

Three days passed when the lamps gave out,
And Caleb Rushton got up and said,
"We've no more water or light or bread,
So we'll live on songs and hope instead,
Live on songs and hope instead."

Listen for the shouts of the black-face miners,
Listen through the rubble for the rescue teams,
Three hundred tons of coal and slag,
Hope imprisoned in a three-foot seam,
Hope imprisoned in a three-foot seam.

Twelve days passed and some were rescued,
Leaving the dead to lie alone,
Through all their lives they dug a grave,
Two miles of earth for a marking stone,
Two miles of earth for a marking stone.

www.ingramcontent.com/pod-product-compliance
Ingram Content Group UK Ltd.
Pitfield, Milton Keynes, MK11 3LW, UK
UKHW062314290726
14090UKWH00018B/1064